For and Against

AN ORAL PRACTICE BOOK
FOR ADVANCED STUDENTS OF ENGLISH

By the same author

SIXTY STEPS TO PRÉCIS
POETRY AND PROSE APPRECIATION
ESSAY AND LETTER-WRITING
A FIRST BOOK IN COMPREHENSION PRÉCIS AND COMPOSITION
THE CARTERS OF GREENWOOD *(Cineloops)*
DETECTIVES FROM SCOTLAND YARD *(Longman Structural Readers, Stage 1)*
CAR THIEVES *(Longman Structural Readers, Stage 1)*
WORTH A FORTUNE *(Longman Structural Readers, Stage 2)*
APRIL FOOLS' DAY *(Longman Structural Readers, Stage 2)*
PROFESSOR BOFFIN'S UMBRELLA *(Longman Structural Readers, Stage 2)*
OPERATION MASTERMIND *(Longman Structural Readers, Stage 3)*
QUESTION AND ANSWER: Graded Aural/Oral Exercises
READING AND WRITING ENGLISH-A First Year Programme for Children
LOOK, LISTEN AND LEARN! Sets 1-4 An Integrated Course for Children
NEW CONCEPT ENGLISH. Sets 1-5 An Integrated Course for Adults and Secondary Students

For and Against

AN ORAL PRACTICE BOOK
FOR ADVANCED STUDENTS OF ENGLISH

L. G. ALEXANDER

Langenscheidt-Longman
ENGLISH LANGUAGE TEACHING

© Longman Group Ltd (formerly
Longmans, Green & Co Ltd) 1968

All rights reserved. No part of this publication may be
reproduced, stored in a retrieval system, or transmitted
in any form or by any means, electronic, mechanical,
photocopying, recording, or otherwise, without
the prior permission of the Copyright owner.

First published 1968

Printed in Germany by
Graph. Betriebe Langenscheidt, Berchtesgaden/Obb.

ISBN 3-526-52306-1

Contents

TO THE TEACHER   page 1

1 It's high time men ceased to regard women as second-class
   citizens   6
2 World governments should conduct serious campaigns against
   smoking   8
3 Television is doing irreparable harm   10
4 Any form of education other than co-education is simply
   unthinkable   12
5 Camping is the ideal way of spending a holiday   14
6 New fashions in clothing are created solely for the commercial
   exploitation of women   16
7 We should all grow fat and be happy   18
8 The younger generation knows best   20
9 Only stricter traffic laws can prevent accidents   22
10 Parents are too permissive with their children nowadays   24
11 Advertisers perform a useful service to the community   26
12 Pop stars certainly earn their money   28
13 Vicious and dangerous sports should be banned by law   30
14 Transistor radios should be prohibited in public places   32
15 The only thing people are interested in today is earning more
   money   34
16 Compulsory military service should be abolished in all countries   36
17 Childhood is certainly not the happiest time of your life   38
18 Untidy people are not nice to know   40
19 The only way to travel is on foot   42
20 Examinations exert a pernicious influence on education   44
21 Books, plays and films should be censored   46
22 People should be rewarded according to ability, not according to
   age and experience   48
23 The tourist trade contributes absolutely nothing to increasing
   understanding between nations   50
24 Only a madman would choose to live in a large modern city   52

25	Equality of opportunity in the twentieth century has not destroyed the class system	54
26	No one wants to live to be a hundred	56
27	Capital punishment is the only way to deter criminals	58
28	The space race is the world's biggest money waster	60
29	Violence can do nothing to diminish race prejudice	62
30	The most important of all human qualities is a sense of humour	64

FORTY ADDITIONAL TOPICS 66

> The arguments put forward in these essays do not necessarily reflect the personal opinions of the author.

To the Teacher

THE CONVERSATION LESSON

In most advanced English courses, time is usually set aside for conversation lessons. These can be the most difficult and most unrewarding of all the lessons the teacher is called upon to conduct. The root of the trouble is that the teacher cannot predict the course of each lesson. He sets a topic and then attempts to stimulate a class discussion by asking questions, suggesting ideas and so on. How the students will respond depends very much on their maturity, general knowledge, range of interests and command of English. It depends, too, on personal factors like shyness or sociability, etc., and even on such things as the time of day and the mood of the class. With some classes, teachers may find that they fail to get any response at all and are finally driven to abandon conversation lessons altogether. With others, the conversation may always be dominated by one or two students, while the teacher spends most of his time coaxing reluctant members of the class to join in. Whatever the case, the conversation lesson tends to be a random, unprogrammed affair over which the teacher has little control. More often than not, time is needlessly frittered away and nothing effective is added to the student's knowledge and skill.

BASIC AIMS

This book seeks to meet most of the problems posed by the advanced conversation lesson by providing a flexible programme which the teacher can manipulate according to the needs of his class. The book contains material which can be used for routine drill work with an unresponsive class, or conversely, the teacher may use it as a source book for ideas and vocabulary with a highly responsive class. The basic aim behind the book is to enable the teacher to predict, to a certain extent, the course of each lesson and to ensure that it will be suited to the requirements of his students.

More specifically, the book provides material which can be used for the following:

                Aural/Oral Comprehension
                Reading Aloud
                Oral Composition
                Class Discussion

FOR WHOM THE BOOK IS INTENDED

This book should be found suitable for:

1   Secondary or adult students who are preparing for the Cambridge

Proficiency in English Examination. The book may be used in addition to an advanced course like *Fluency in English*.

2 Secondary or adult students who are not preparing for an examination of any kind and who are attending classes mainly to improve their command of spoken English.

3 Schools and institutes where 'wastage' caused by irregular attendance and late starters is a problem.

ASSUMED AURAL/ORAL ABILITY

Students who have completed elementary and intermediate courses in spoken English should have no difficulty with this book. *For and Against* may be used to follow up any of the following:

Conversation Exercises in Everyday English (Jerrom and Szkutnik)
Question and Answer (Alexander)
The Carters of Greenwood (Cineloops) Elementary and Intermediate Levels (Alexander)

In any case, the following skills have been assumed:

1 The ability to understand English dealing with everyday subjects and spoken at normal speed.
2 The ability to answer questions which require short or extended answers.
3 The ability to ask questions to elicit short or extended answers.
4 The ability to use orally a large number of elementary and intermediate sentence patterns.
5 The ability to reproduce orally the substance of a passage of English (narrative and descriptive prose) after having heard it several times and read it.
6 The ability to conduct a simple conversation on everyday subjects (e.g. expressing preferences; polite interchange; careers; travel; common experiences, etc.).
7 The ability to give a short talk (prepared or unprepared) lasting up to five minutes on everyday subjects.
8 The ability to read a passage of English aloud. The student should have a fair grasp of the rhythm of the language (stress and intonation) even if he is unable to pronounce unfamiliar words correctly.
9 The ability to read silently and understand works of fiction and non-fiction of the level of Longmans' Bridge Series. The student's passive vocabulary should be in the region of 3000 words (*structural* and *lexical*). The student should be sufficiently familiar with a wide variety of English sentence patterns so that he can 'get the gist' of what he is reading even though he may not know the meaning of individual words.

A DESCRIPTION OF THE MATERIAL

Layout

For and Against consists of thirty exercises each one of which is laid out on facing pages. An argumentative essay always appears on the left-hand page; and two sets of notes appear on the right-hand page.

Left-hand Pages: The Passages

Each essay is approximately 500 words in length and argues in favour of a proposition. The passages are not academic essays; they are light, informal and conversational in style. Only one side of the case is presented and the argument is often deliberately provocative and even bigoted and extremist. The intention is to motivate the students by any means — even by making them angry — and spark off a spontaneous debate in the classroom. The thirty essays cover a wide range of subjects of general interest, some serious, some light-hearted. Most of the topics have been tried out with considerable success on mixed classes of adult students. With regard to the subject-matter, it has been assumed that the student reads newspapers (either in his own language or in English) and takes an interest in topics which are frequently discussed in the papers, in magazines, and on radio and television programmes. The passages are not graded at all linguistically, but roughly in terms of intellectual content, the more difficult subjects being presented in the latter part of the book.

Right-hand Pages: The Notes

Each right-hand page is divided into two parts. The top half consists of a list of numbered 'key words' and notes summarising the argument put forward in the essay. The lower half of the page consists of 'key words' and notes summarising the counter-argument: this information is *not* derived from the essay. Brackets appear beside the notes. These are intended to catch the student's eye when he is speaking impromptu from the notes. The brackets conveniently group together the main sub-divisions in the argument and counter-argument and may be found useful for round-the-class exercises as well.

Additional Topics

A list of forty additional topics appears at the end of the book.

HOW TO USE THIS BOOK

The teacher is obviously free to use the material in any way that best suits his class. In general, it may be said that the less responsive the class is, the more it will be necessary to adopt a fixed routine. With highly articulate classes, the essays and notes may be referred to as source material. Even with articulate classes, however, some teachers prefer to adopt a fixed routine.

The ideas given below should be treated as suggestions only. The following procedure is recommended:

(*a*) **Listening (books shut)**
(*b*) **Listening and understanding (books open)**

(c) Listening (books shut)
(d) Reading aloud (books open)
(e) Answering mixed questions (books shut)
(f) Asking mixed questions (books shut)
(g) Oral composition (books open)
(h) Class discussion or debate (books open)

In practice, this would work as follows:

(a) *Listening (books shut)*
The teacher reads the passage once. The students listen only and try to understand as much as they can at first hearing.

(b) *Listening and understanding (books open)*
The teacher reads the passage again, stopping at convenient points to explain unfamiliar words and constructions. Rather than give direct explanations, he tries to elicit as much information as possible from the students. Explanations should be given entirely in English. Translation into the students' mother-tongue may, on occasion, be used as a last resort and then only to translate lexical items, not patterns. The teacher must ensure that the students understand the text completely before proceeding to the next part of the lesson. The students must, of course, read the text silently while the teacher is going through it.

(c) *Listening (books shut)*
The teacher reads the passage once more. The students should now be in a position to understand all of it.

(d) *Reading aloud (books open)*
Individual students are now asked to read small sections of the passage. This is done quickly round the class.

(e) *Answering mixed questions (books shut)*
The teacher asks questions about the passage to elicit short or extended answers. The questions are asked rapidly round the class.

(f) *Asking mixed questions (books shut)*
The teacher may get the students to ask each other questions about the passage, or he may choose to elicit questions in the following manner:

Teacher: Ask me if it was printed in the papers.
Student: Was it printed in the papers?
Teacher: When ...
Student: When was it printed in the papers? etc.

N.B. If time is short, or if the students are quite proficient at answering and asking questions, sections (e) and (f) may be omitted.

(g) Oral composition (books open)
The students may be asked to work in two ways:

1 The students refer to the key words of the argument which appear on the top half of the facing page. Individual students are asked to reconstruct the argument, or part of the argument, by referring only to the key words. The bracketed notes will be found useful for this purpose. At a later stage, when the students have made some progress, they may be asked to make their own notes of the argument and to compare them with the key words before attempting oral reconstruction.

2 The students are then asked to refer to the key words of the counter-argument on the lower half of the facing page. Individual students are asked to construct the counter-argument orally by referring only to the key words.

(h) Class discussion or debate (books open)
The topic presented in the passage is now thrown open to the whole class and is discussed. During the discussion, members of the class may draw freely on the ideas 'for' and 'against' which are summarised in note form. They should also, if possible, contribute ideas of their own.

Teachers may sometimes choose to conduct a full-scale debate as this unfailingly adds spice and excitement to the lesson. One member of class may be appointed to act as chairman and two main speakers may be called upon to present their cases before the class participates in the discussion. A vote may be cast at the end of the debate, though as is usual in debates, the students should be asked to vote only on the quality of the arguments they have heard. The way they vote need not necessarily be consistent with their personal views.

ALLOCATION OF TIME

A conversation lesson falling into the eight distinct stages described above may be conducted in an hour or an hour and a half, depending on the size of the class. If one session a week is devoted to aural/oral work, the material in the book will be completed in a year.

OTHER POSSIBLE USES

Though it is primarily intended for oral practice, this book may be put to a variety of other uses. For instance, the teacher may occasionally give dictation exercises, or the students may be asked to draw on the notes to write argumentative compositions as homework. Alternatively, the students may be asked to write a reported speech summary of the class debate or discussion. Written exercises of this kind may be found useful in consolidating aural/oral work done in the classroom. Some teachers may also find the passages suitable for speed reading tests.

1 'It's high time men ceased to regard women as second-class citizens'

This is supposed to be an enlightened age, but you wouldn't think so if you could hear what the average man thinks of the average woman. Women won their independence years ago. After a long, bitter struggle, they now enjoy the same educational opportunities as men in most parts of the world. They have proved repeatedly that they are equal and often superior to men in almost every field. The hard-fought battle for recognition has been won, but it is by no means over. It is men, not women who still carry on the sex war because their attitude remains basically hostile. Even in the most progressive societies, women continue to be regarded as second-rate citizens. To hear some men talk, you'd think that women belonged to a different species!

On the surface, the comments made by men about women's abilities seem light-hearted. The same tired jokes about women drivers are repeated day in, day out. This apparent light-heartedness does not conceal the real contempt that men feel for women. However much men sneer at women, their claims to superiority are not borne out by statistics. Let's consider the matter of driving, for instance. We all know that women cause far fewer accidents than men. They are too conscientious and responsible to drive like maniacs. But this is a minor quibble. Women have succeeded in any job you care to name. As politicians, soldiers, doctors, factory-hands, university professors, farmers, company directors, lawyers, bus-conductors, scientists and presidents of countries they have often put men to shame. And we must remember that they frequently succeed brilliantly in all these fields *in addition to* bearing and rearing children.

Yet men go on maintaining the fiction that there are many jobs women can't do. Top-level political negotiation between countries, business and banking are almost entirely controlled by men, who jealously guard their so-called 'rights'. Even in otherwise enlightened places like Switzerland women haven't even been given the vote. This situation is preposterous! The arguments that men put forward to exclude women from these fields are all too familiar. Women, they say, are unreliable and irrational. They depend too little on cool reasoning and too much on intuition and instinct to arrive at decisions. They are not even capable of thinking clearly. Yet when women prove their abilities, men refuse to acknowledge them and give them their due. So much for a man's ability to think clearly!

The truth is that men cling to their supremacy because of their basic inferiority complex. They shun real competition. They know in their hearts that women are superior and they are afraid of being beaten at their own game. One of the most important tasks in the world is to achieve peace between the nations. You can be sure that if women were allowed to sit round the conference table, they would succeed brilliantly, as they always do, where men have failed for centuries. Some things are too important to be left to men!

The argument: key words

1. Supposed to be enlightened age: not really so.
2. Women won independence years ago.
3. Long struggle: equal educational opportunities as men.
4. Proved repeatedly: equal, often superior to men in every field.
5. Battle not over: men carry on sex war; basically hostile.
6. Even in progressive societies: women second-rate citizens; different species!
7. Light-hearted comments made by men: e.g. women drivers.
8. Does not conceal real contempt; but statistics disprove their claims.
9. Take driving: women: fewer accidents; responsible drivers, not maniacs.
10. Success in any job: politicians, etc. – bear and rear children as well.
11. Men maintain fiction: women can't do certain jobs.
12. E.g. top-level political negotiation, banking, no vote in certain countries.
13. Why? Familiar arguments: women unreliable, irrational, depend on instinct, intuition.
14. Men refuse to acknowledge proven ability. Clear thinking?
15. Men cling to supremacy: inferiority complex.
16. Shun competition; may be beaten.
17. Most important task: world peace.
18. Success if negotiations by women; some things too important to be done by men.

The counter-argument: key words

1. Women: militant, shout louder because they have weak case.
2. Even now, they still talk like suffragettes.
3. It's nonsense to claim that men and women are equal and have the same abilities.
4. Women: different biological function; physically weaker; different, not inferior, intellectually.
5. Impossible to be wives, mothers *and* successful career women.
6. Really *are* unreliable: employers can't trust them. Not their fault: leave jobs to get married, have children.
7. Great deal of truth in light-hearted jokes: e.g. women drivers. Women: less practical, less mechanically-minded.
8. Most women *glad* to let men look after important affairs.
9. They know that bearing and rearing children are more important.
10. That's why there are few women in politics, etc. They are not excluded; they exclude themselves.
11. Anyway, we live in woman-dominated societies: e.g. USA, Western Europe.
12. Who is the *real* boss in the average household? Certainly not father!
13. Men are second-class citizens and women should grant them equal status!

2 'World governments should conduct serious campaigns against smoking'

If you smoke and you still don't believe that there's a definite link between smoking and bronchial troubles, heart disease and lung cancer, then you are certainly deceiving yourself. No one will accuse you of hypocrisy. Let us just say that you are suffering from a bad case of wishful thinking. This needn't make you too uncomfortable because you are in good company. Whenever the subject of smoking and health is raised, the goverments of most countries hear no evil, see no evil and smell no evil. Admittedly, a few governments have taken timid measures. In Britain, for instance, cigarette advertising has been banned on television. The conscience of the nation is appeased, while the population continues to puff its way to smoky, cancerous death.

You don't have to look very far to find out why the official reactions to medical findings have been so luke-warm. The answer is simply money. Tobacco is a wonderful commodity to tax. It's almost like a tax on our daily bread. In tax revenue alone, the government of Britain collects enough from smokers to pay for its entire educational facilities. So while the authorities point out ever so discreetly that smoking may, conceivably, be harmful, it doesn't do to shout too loudly about it.

This is surely the most short-sighted policy you could imagine. While money is eagerly collected in vast sums with one hand, it is paid out in increasingly vaster sums with the other. Enormous amounts are spent on cancer research and on efforts to cure people suffering from the disease. Countless valuable lives are lost. In the long run, there is no doubt that everybody would be much better-off if smoking were banned altogether.

Of course, we are not ready for such drastic action. But if the governments of the world were honestly concerned about the welfare of their peoples, you'd think they'd conduct aggressive anti-smoking campaigns. Far from it! The tobacco industry is allowed to spend staggering sums on advertising. Its advertising is as insidious as it is dishonest. We are never shown pictures of real smokers coughing up their lungs early in the morning. That would never do. The advertisements always depict virile, clean-shaven young men. They suggest it is manly to smoke, even positively healthy! Smoking is associated with the great open-air life, with beautiful girls, true love and togetherness. What utter nonsense!

For a start, governments could begin by banning all cigarette and tobacco advertising and should then conduct anti-smoking advertising campaigns of their own. Smoking should be banned in all public places like theatres, cinemas and restaurants. Great efforts should be made to inform young people especially of the dire consequences of taking up the habit. A horrific warning – say, a picture of a death's head – should be included in every packet of cigarettes that is sold. As individuals we are certainly weak, but if governments acted honestly and courageously, they could protect us from ourselves.

The argument: key words

1. Definite link: smoking and bronchial troubles, heart disease, lung cancer.
2. Governments hear, see, smell no evil.
3. A few governments: timid measures.
4. E.g. Britain: TV advertising banned; nation's conscience appeased; cancerous death.
5. Official reactions to medical findings: luke-warm.
6. Tobacco: source of revenue. E.g. Britain: tobacco tax pays for education.
7. A short-sighted policy.
8. Enormous sums spent fighting the disease; lives lost.
9. Smoking should be banned altogether.
10. We are not ready for such drastic action.
11. But governments, if really concerned, should conduct aggressive anti-smoking campaigns.
12. The tobacco industry spends vast sums on advertising.
13. Advertising: insidious, dishonest.
14. Never shown pictures of real smokers coughing up lungs, only virile young men.
15. Smoking associated with great open-air life, beautiful girls, togetherness. Nonsense!
16. All advertising should be banned; anti-smoking campaign conducted.
17. Smoking should be banned in public places.
18. Young people should be warned, dire consequences.
19. Warning, death's head, included in every packet.
20. Governments should protect us from ourselves.

The counter-argument: key words

1. There are still scientists who doubt smoking/cancer link.
2. People who don't smoke should keep quiet.
3. Smoking brings many psychological benefits:
4. Relieves stresses of everyday life: provides constant consolation.
5. E.g. we smoke when taking exams, worried, bereaved, etc.
6. Associated with good living; social contacts made easier.
7. Smoking is very enjoyable: relaxing, e.g. with a cup of coffee; after a meal, etc.
8. It's absurd to suggest we ban it after so many hundreds of years.
9. Enormous interests involved: governments, tobacco growers, tobacco industries, retail businesses.
10. Tax apart, important source of income to many countries: e.g. USA, Rhodesia, Greece, Turkey.
11. People should be free to decide, not bullied by governments; banning is undemocratic.
12. The tobacco industry spends vast sums on medical research.
13. Improved filters have resulted; e.g. Columbia University.
14. Now possible to smoke and enjoy it without danger.

3 'Television is doing irreparable harm'

'Yes, but what did we use to *do* before there was television?' How often we hear statements like this! Television hasn't been with us all that long, but we are already beginning to forget what the world was like without it. Before we admitted the one-eyed monster into our homes, we never found it difficult to occupy our spare time. We used to enjoy civilised pleasures. For instance, we used to have hobbies, we used to entertain our friends and be entertained by them, we used to go outside for our amusements to theatres, cinemas, restaurants and sporting events. We even used to read books and listen to music and broadcast talks occasionally. All that belongs to the past. Now all our free time is regulated by the 'goggle box'. We rush home or gulp down our meals to be in time for this or that programme. We have even given up sitting at table and having a leisurely evening meal, exchanging the news of the day. A sandwich and a glass of beer will do – anything, providing it doesn't interfere with the programme. The monster demands and obtains absolute silence and attention. If any member of the family dares to open his mouth during a programme, he is quickly silenced.

Whole generations are growing up addicted to the telly. Food is left uneaten, homework undone and sleep is lost. The telly is a universal pacifier. It is now standard practice for mother to keep the children quiet by putting them in the living-room and turning on the set. It doesn't matter that the children will watch rubbishy commercials or spectacles of sadism and violence – so long as they are quiet.

There is a limit to the amount of creative talent available in the world. Every day, television consumes vast quantities of creative work. That is why most of the programmes are so bad: it is impossible to keep pace with the demand and maintain high standards as well. When millions watch the same programmes, the whole world becomes a village, and society is reduced to the conditions which obtain in pre-literate communities. We become utterly dependent on the two most primitive media of communication: pictures and the spoken word.

Television encourages passive enjoyment. We become content with second-hand experiences. It is so easy to sit in our armchairs watching others working. Little by little, television cuts us off from the real world. We get so lazy, we choose to spend a fine day in semi-darkness, glued to our sets, rather than go out into the world itself. Television may be a splendid medium of communication, but it prevents us from communicating with each other. We only become aware how totally irrelevant television is to real living when we spend a holiday by the sea or in the mountains, far away from civilisation. In quiet, natural surroundings, we quickly discover how little we miss the hypnotic tyranny of King Telly.

The argument: key words

1. Beginning to forget what we did before television.
2. Always occupied our spare time; enjoyed civilised pleasures.
3. E.g. hobbies, entertaining, outside amusements: theatres, etc.
4. Even used to read books, listen to music, broadcast talks.
5. Free time now regulated by television.
6. Rush home, gulp food; sandwich, glass of beer.
7. Monster demands: absolute silence and attention; daren't open your mouth.
8. Whole generations growing up addicted; neglect other things.
9. Universal pacifier: mother and children.
10. Children exposed to rubbishy commercials, violence, etc.
11. Limit to creative talent available.
12. Therefore many bad programmes; can't keep pace with demand.
13. World becomes a village; pre-literate society; dependent on pictures and words.
14. Passive enjoyment; second-hand experiences; sit in armchairs, others working.
15. Cut off from real world.
16. Become lazy, glued to sets instead of going out.
17. Television totally irrelevant to real living.
18. E.g. holiday, natural surroundings; never miss hypnotic tyranny.

The counter-argument: key words

1. Nobody imposes TV on you. If you don't like it, don't buy a set – or switch off!
2. We are free to enjoy 'civilised pleasures' and still do.
3. Only when there is lack of moderation can TV be bad – true for all things.
4. People sometimes feel guilty watching TV; absurd idea.
5. If you boast you don't watch TV, it's like boasting you don't read books.
6. Must watch to be well-informed.
7. Considerable variety of programmes; can select what we want to see.
8. Continuous cheap source of information and entertainment.
9. Enormous possibilities for education: e.g. close-circuit TV – surgery.
10. Schools broadcasts; educating adult illiterates; specialised subjects: e.g. language teaching.
11. Education in broadest sense: ideals of democracy; political argument, etc.
12. Provides outlet for creative talents.
13. Many playwrights, actors, etc., emerged from TV.
14. Vast potential still waiting to be exploited: colour TV; world network: communication via satellite.
15. TV is a unifying force in the world.

4 'Any form of education other than co-education is simply unthinkable'

Imagine being asked to spend twelve or so years of your life in a society which consisted only of members of your own sex. How would you react? Unless there was something definitely wrong with you, you wouldn't be too happy about it, to say the least. It is all the more surprising therefore that so many parents in the world choose to impose such abnormal conditions on their children – conditions which they themselves wouldn't put up with for one minute!

Any discussion of this topic is bound to question the aims of education. Stuffing children's heads full of knowledge is far from being foremost among them. One of the chief aims of education is to equip future citizens with all they require to take their place in adult society. Now adult society is made up of men and women, so how can a segregated school possibly offer the right sort of preparation for it? Anyone entering adult society after years of segregation can only be in for a shock.

A co-educational school offers children nothing less than a true version of society in miniature. Boys and girls are given the opportunity to get to know each other, to learn to live together from their earliest years. They are put in a position where they can compare themselves with each other in terms of academic ability, athletic achievement and many of the extracurricular activities which are part of school life. What a practical advantage it is (to give just a small example) to be able to put on a school play in which the male parts will be taken by boys and the female parts by girls! What nonsense co-education makes of the argument that boys are cleverer than girls or vice-versa. When segregated, boys and girls are made to feel that they are a race apart. Rivalry between the sexes is fostered. In a co-educational school, everything falls into its proper place.

But perhaps the greatest contribution of co-education is the healthy attitude to life it encourages. Boys don't grow up believing that women are mysterious creatures – airy goddesses, more like book-illustrations to a fairy-tale, than human beings. Girls don't grow up imagining that men are romantic heroes. Years of living together at school dispel illusions of this kind. There are no goddesses with freckles, pigtails, piercing voices and inky fingers. There are no romantic heroes with knobbly knees, dirty fingernails and unkempt hair. The awkward stage of adolescence brings into sharp focus some of the physical and emotional problems involved in growing up. These can better be overcome in a co-educational environment. Segregated schools sometimes provide the right conditions for sexual deviation. This is hardly possible under a co-educational system. When the time comes for the pupils to leave school, they are fully prepared to enter society as well-adjusted adults. They have already had years of experience in coping with many of the problems that face men and women.

The argument: key words

1. Imagine spending 12 years with members of own sex. Reactions? – wouldn't enjoy it.
2. Many parents impose these conditions on their children.
3. Discussion of topic must question aims of education.
4. Not only accumulation of knowledge.
5. Equipping future citizens for adult society.
6. Segregated schools: not the right sort of preparation.
7. Co-educational school: society in miniature.
8. Boys and girls learning to live together.
9. Can compare themselves: academic and athletic abilities; school activities.
10. Many practical advantages: e.g. school plays.
11. Boys and girls not made to feel a race apart.
12. Co-education encourages healthy attitudes to life.
13. Boys: no illusions about women: airy goddesses.
14. Girls: no illusions about men: romantic heroes.
15. No goddesses with freckles, pigtails, piercing voices, etc.
16. No romantic heroes with knobbly knees, dirty fingernails, etc.
17. Physical and emotional adolescent problems best overcome in co-educational environment.
18. Sexual deviation hardly possible.
19. Pupils enter society as well-adjusted adults.

The counter-argument: key words

1. School is not a miniature society.
2. It is highly artificial; unrelated to outside world.
3. It is a training ground: a very special society in its own right.
4. Many teachers claim better work done in segregated schools.
5. Greater achievements academically, socially, in athletics, etc.
6. Children from segregated schools have greater self-confidence when they leave.
7. Many more practical advantages in segregated schools: e.g. administration.
8. Adolescent problems better dealt with – easier for teachers to handle.
9. Sexual deviations, greatly exaggerated.
10. No distractions – co-educational schools often lead to disastrous early marriages.
11. Segregated schools have successfully existed for centuries: a proof of their worth.
12. In many countries, the most famous schools are segregated.
13. Thousands of great men and women attended segregated schools: e.g. Churchill.

5 'Camping is the ideal way of spending a holiday'

There was a time when camping was considered to be a poor way of spending a holiday: OK for boy scouts and hard-up students, but hardly the thing for sophisticated, comfort-loving adults. The adults have at last discovered that the boy scouts have really been on to a good thing all these years. If you go camping, it no longer means that you will be bitten to death by mosquitoes; have to drink brackish coffee; live on corned beef; suffocate or freeze in a sleeping-bag; hump gargantuan weights on your back. Camping has become the great pursuit of motorists the world over. All the discomforts associated with it have been miraculously whisked away. For a modest outlay, you can have a comfortable, insulated tent. For a not-so-modest outlay, you can have an elaborate affair which resembles a portable bungalow, complete with three bedrooms, a living-room, a kitchen and a porch. The portable furniture is light and comfortable; the gas stove brews excellent coffee or grills a tender steak; the refrigerator keeps the beer and ice-cream cold; and as for a good night's rest, well, you literally sleep on air. What more could you want?

No wonder the great rush is on. You see, camping has so much to offer. You enjoy absolute freedom. You have none of the headaches of advance hotel booking or driving round and round a city at midnight looking for a room. There are no cold hotel breakfasts, no surly staff to tip. For a ludicrously small sum, you can enjoy comforts which few hotels could provide. Modern camping sites are well equipped with hot and cold running water and even shops and dance floors! Low-cost holidays make camping an attractive proposition. But above all, you enjoy tremendous mobility. If you don't like a place, or if it is too crowded, you can simply get up and go. Conversely, you can stay as long as you like. You're the boss.

And then there's the sheer fun of it – especially if you have a family. Moping around a stuffy hotel room wondering what they are going to give you for dinner is a tedious business. By comparison, it's so exciting to arrive at a camp site, put up your tent and start getting a meal ready. You are active all the time and you are always close to nature. Imagine yourself beside some clear stream with mountains in the background. Night is falling, everything is peaceful – except for the delightful sound of chops sizzling in the pan! Camping provides you with a *real* change from everyday living. You get up earlier, go to bed earlier, develop a hearty appetite. You have enormous opportunity to meet people of various nationalities and to share your pleasures with them. People are so friendly when they are relaxed. How remote the strained world of hotels seems when you are camping! How cold and unfriendly the formal greetings that are exchanged each day between the residents! For a few precious weeks in the year, you really adopt a completely different way of life. And that's the essence of true recreation and real enjoyment.

The argument: key words

1. Camping once considered poor way of spending holiday: boy scouts; students; no longer so.
2. No inconveniences (e.g. mosquitoes; brackish coffee; corned beef; freeze, suffocate in sleeping-bag; hump great weights).
3. Pursuit of motorists everywhere: no discomforts.
4. Modest sum: insulated tent.
5. Large sum: portable bungalow; three bedrooms, kitchen, etc.
6. Portable furniture: gas stove: coffee, steak; refrigerator: beer, ice-cream.
7. Sleep on air.
8. The great rush is on; camping offers absolute freedom.
9. No advance hotel booking; driving round cities at midnight.
10. Low cost holidays; many comforts at modern sites: e.g. hot, cold water, even dance floors!
11. Great mobility: go or stay as you please.
12. Sheer fun of it: especially with family.
13. No moping round hotel rooms wondering about dinner.
14. Exciting to arrive at site, put up tent; prepare meal.
15. Always active; always close to nature.
16. Imagine clear stream; mountains; chops sizzling in pan.
17. A real change: get up early, go to bed early; hearty appetite.
18. Great opportunity to meet people; everyone relaxed, friendly.
19. Adopt completely different way of life: essence of relaxation, enjoyment.

The counter-argument: key words

1. Argument doesn't mention any inconveniences.
2. What about rain, cold, mosquitoes, boring diet of fried food?
3. What about packing and re-erecting a wet tent?
4. What about vast number of things to be carried? Large car necessary.
5. Frequently setting up and disbanding house: enormously inconvenient and tedious.
6. Most real beauty spots are inaccessible by car: everything must be carried.
7. The real beauty spots have no amenities, not even running water.
8. Camping sites are not beauty spots: primitive living conditions; like ugly slums; each camper has little space.
9. Many official sites haven't even primitive amenities.
10. Camping sites can be just as crowded as hotels.
11. Camping is not a real holiday for the family.
12. Wife has to cook, etc., under primitive conditions; no change for her.
13. Husband must drive long distances; children get tired.
14. Even cheapest and simplest hotel provides rest and freedom from care for *everyone* in the family.
15. You get what you pay for; when camping, you don't pay much and and don't get much.

6 'New fashions in clothing are created solely for the commercial exploitation of women'

Whenever you see an old film, even one made as little as ten years ago, you cannot help being struck by the appearance of the women taking part. Their hair-styles and make-up look dated; their skirts look either too long or too short; their general appearance is, in fact, slightly ludicrous. The men taking part in the film, on the other hand, are clearly recognisable. There is nothing about their appearance to suggest that they belong to an entirely different age.

This illusion is created by changing fashions. Over the years, the great majority of men have successfully resisted all attempts to make them change their style of dress. The same cannot be said for women. Each year a few so-called 'top designers' in Paris or London lay down the law and women the whole world over rush to obey. The decrees of the designers are unpredictable and dictatorial. This year, they decide in their arbitrary fashion, skirts will be short and waists will be high; zips are *in* and buttons are *out*. Next year the law is reversed and far from taking exception, no one is even mildly surprised.

If women are mercilessly exploited year after year, they have only themselves to blame. Because they shudder at the thought of being seen in public in clothes that are out of fashion, they are annually blackmailed by the designers and the big stores. Clothes which have been worn only a few times have to be discarded because of the dictates of fashion. When you come to think of it, only a woman is capable of standing in front of a wardrobe packed full of clothes and announcing sadly that she has nothing to wear.

Changing fashions are nothing more than the deliberate creation of waste. Many women squander vast sums of money each year to replace clothes that have hardly been worn. Women who cannot afford to discard clothing in this way, waste hours of their time altering the dresses they have. Hem-lines are taken up or let down; waist-lines are taken in or let out; neck-lines are lowered or raised, and so on.

No one can claim that the fashion industry contributes anything really important to society. Fashion designers are rarely concerned with vital things like warmth, comfort and durability. They are only interested in outward appearance and they take advantage of the fact that women will put up with any amount of discomfort, providing they look right. There can hardly be a man who hasn't at some time in his life smiled at the sight of a woman shivering in a flimsy dress on a wintry day, or delicately picking her way through deep snow in dainty shoes.

When comparing men and women in the matter of fashion, the conclusions to be drawn are obvious. Do the constantly changing fashions of women's clothes, one wonders, reflect basic qualities of fickleness and instability? Men are too sensible to let themselves be bullied by fashion designers. Do their unchanging styles of dress reflect basic qualities of stability and reliability? That is for you to decide.

The argument: key words

1. In old films women look odd: hair-styles, make-up, dress.
2. Men, clearly recognisable; don't belong to different age.

3. This illusion created by changing fashions.
4. Most men have resisted fashion, but not women.
5. Top designers, Paris, London, lay down law; dictatorial.
6. One year, one thing; next year the reverse; no one is surprised.

7. Women mercilessly exploited; they are to blame.
8. Afraid to be seen in public in old-fashioned clothes.
9. Blackmailed by designers, big stores.
10. New clothes discarded; wardrobe full, but nothing to wear.

11. Changing fashions: the deliberate creation of waste.
12. Women waste money: throw away new clothes. Waste time: alter hem-lines, waist-lines, neck-lines, etc.

13. The fashion industry contributes nothing to society.
14. Designers not interested in important things: warmth, comfort, durability.
15. Interested only in outward appearance.
16. Women put up with great discomfort: e.g. winter.

17. Comparing men and women: obvious conclusions to be drawn.
18. Women: fickle, unstable?
19. Men, not bullied by designers, stable, reliable? You decide.

The counter-argument: key words

1. Fashion adds spice to life: colour, variety, beauty.
2. Women follow fashions to please themselves – and men!
3. The world a dull place if women always wore the same clothes.

4. There is no commercial exploitation: a huge demand for new styles always exists.
5. Mass production makes well-designed clothes cheap, available to everyone.

6. These days, men are fashion-conscious too: hair-styles, shirts, suits, shoes, etc.
7. Men in drab unimaginative clothes rapidly becoming a minority.
8. It's nonsense to draw conclusions about male–female characteristics from attitudes to fashion; only a man would do that.

9. Changing fashion is *not* the deliberate creation of waste.
10. Enormous industry, providing employment for vast numbers: e.g. sheep farmers, designers, textile mills, stores, etc.
11. Industrial research: new materials: nylon, rayon, terylene, etc.
12. Huge import–export business, important to world trade.

13. Psychological importance of being well-dressed: confidence in one's appearance very important.
14. Fashion contributes a great deal to society.

7 'We should all grow fat and be happy'

Here's a familiar version of the boy-meets-girl situation. A young man has at last plucked up courage to invite a dazzling young lady out to dinner. She has accepted his invitation and he is overjoyed. He is determined to take her to the best restaurant in town, even if it means that he will have to live on memories and hopes during the month to come. When they get to the restaurant, he discovers that this etherial creature is on a diet. She mustn't eat this and she mustn't drink that. Oh, but of course, she doesn't want to spoil *his* enjoyment. Let him by all means eat as much fattening food as he wants: it's the surest way to an early grave. They spend a truly memorable evening together and never see each other again.

What a miserable lot dieters are! You can always recognise them from the sour expression on their faces. They spend most of their time turning their noses up at food. They are forever consulting calorie charts; gazing at themselves in mirrors; and leaping on to weighing-machines in the bathroom. They spend a lifetime fighting a losing battle against spreading hips, protruding tummies and double chins. Some wage all-out war on FAT. Mere dieting is not enough. They exhaust themselves doing exercises, sweating in sauna baths, being pummelled and massaged by weird machines. The really wealthy diet-mongers pay vast sums for 'health cures'. For two weeks they can enter a 'nature clinic' and be starved to death for a hundred guineas a week. Don't think its only the middle-aged who go in for these fads either. Many of these bright young things you see are suffering from chronic malnutrition: they are living on nothing but air, water and the goodwill of God.

Dieters undertake to starve themselves of their own free will so why are they so miserable? Well, for one thing, they're always hungry. You can't be hungry *and* happy at the same time. All the horrible concoctions they eat instead of food leave them permanently dissatisfied. 'Wonderfood is a *complete* food,' the advertisement says. 'Just dissolve a teaspoonful in water....' A complete food it may be, but not quite as complete as a juicy steak. And, of course, they're always miserable because they feel so guilty. Hunger just proves too much for them and in the end they lash out and devour five huge guilt-inducing cream cakes at a sitting. And who can blame them? At least three times a day they are exposed to temptation. What utter torture it is always watching others tucking into piles of mouth-watering food while you munch a water biscuit and sip unsweetened lemon juice!

What's all this self-inflicted torture for? Saintly people deprive themselves of food to attain a state of grace. Unsaintly people do so to attain a state of misery. It will be a great day when all the dieters in the world abandon their slimming courses; when they hold out their plates and demand second helpings!

The argument: key words

1. Boy-meets-girl situation: young man invites young lady to dinner.
2. She accepts; he's overjoyed; best restaurant in town.
3. She's on a diet; doesn't want to spoil *his* enjoyment.
4. Memorable evening; never see each other again.

5. Dieters: a miserable lot.
6. Sour expression on faces: always turning noses up at food.
7. Always consulting calorie charts; gazing at mirrors; weighing themselves.
8. Battle against: spreading hips; protruding tummies; double chins.
9. Some: all-out war on fat: exercises, sauna baths, etc.
10. The wealthy: health cures; starve for 100 guineas a week.
11. Not only middle-aged. Bright young things: malnutrition.

12. Dieters miserable because they are always hungry.
13. Eat horrible concoctions; always dissatisfied; e.g. 'Wonderfood' and juicy steak.
14. Feel guilt; hunger proves too much; eat five cream cakes.
15. Exposed to temptation three times a day.
16. Torture watching others eat; water biscuits, lemon juice.

17. Why all this torture?
18. Saints: deprive themselves: a state of grace. Others: a state of misery.
19. A great day when: dieters abandon slimming cures; demand second helpings.

The counter-argument: key words

1. It's a myth that all fat people are happy.
2. Dieters are usually fat people, or have tendency to get fat.
3. Obesity makes them objects of ridicule; miserable at school and as grown-ups.

4. Overweight is bad for health: leads to heart diseases, high blood pressure, etc.
5. Medical science has proved that animal fats, excessive sugar, carbohydrates, etc., are harmful.

6. Fat people therefore suffer psychologically and physically.
7. People diet for a number of very good reasons:
8. The ideal human form is slim.
9. Fat men and women are unattractive to look at.
10. Ready-made clothes are hard to obtain.
11. Fat people tire easily.
12. Insurance companies charge higher premiums.

13. Overeating is common in many societies.
14. Dieting is associated with sensible living.

8 'The younger generation knows best'

Old people are always saying that the young are not what they were. The same comment is made from generation to generation and it is always true. It has never been truer than it is today. The young are better educated. They have a lot more money to spend and enjoy more freedom. They grow up more quickly and are not so dependent on their parents. They think more for themselves and do not blindly accept the ideals of their elders. Events which the older generation remembers vividly are nothing more than past history. This is as it should be. Every new generation is different from the one that preceded it. Today the difference is very marked indeed.

The old always assume that they know best for the simple reason that they have been around a bit longer. They don't like to feel that their values are being questioned or threatened. And this is precisely what the young are doing. They are questioning the assumptions of their elders and disturbing their complacency. They take leave to doubt that the older generation has created the best of all possible worlds. What they reject more than anything is conformity. Office hours, for instance, are nothing more than enforced slavery. Wouldn't people work best if they were given complete freedom and responsibility? And what about clothing? Who said that all the men in the world should wear drab grey suits and convict haircuts? If we turn our minds to more serious matters, who said that human differences can best be solved through conventional politics or by violent means? Why have the older generation so often used violence to solve their problems? Why are they so unhappy and guilt-ridden in their personal lives, so obsessed with mean ambitions and the desire to amass more and more material possessions? Can *anything* be right with the rat-race? Haven't the old lost touch with all that is important in life?

These are not questions the older generation can shrug off lightly. Their record over the past forty years or so hasn't been exactly spotless. Traditionally, the young have turned to their elders for guidance. Today, the situation might be reversed. The old – if they are prepared to admit it – could learn a thing or two from their children. One of the biggest lessons they could learn is that enjoyment is not 'sinful'. Enjoyment is a principle one could apply to all aspects of life. It is surely not wrong to enjoy your work and enjoy your leisure; to shed restricting inhibitions. It is surely not wrong to live in the present rather than in the past or future. This emphasis on the present is only to be expected because the young have grown up under the shadow of the bomb: the constant threat of complete annihilation. This is their glorious heritage. Can we be surprised that they should so often question the sanity of the generation that bequeathed it?

The argument: key words

1. The young are not what they were: always true, generation to generation.
2. Today: the young are better educated; more money, freedom; grow up more quickly; less dependent on parents.
3. Do not blindly accept ideals of elders.
4. Events vividly remembered by older generation: past history.
5. Every generation different; today, difference very marked.
6. The old assume they know best: more experience.
7. The young question values and assumptions; disturb elders' complacency.
8. Old created best of all possible worlds?
9. The young reject conformity; regular office hours; freedom and responsibility are better.
10. Clothing: drab grey suits and convict haircuts best?
11. Serious questions: human differences best solved by conventional politics, violent means?
12. The old: unhappy personal lives; mean ambitions; material possessions.
13. Rat-race: lost touch with important things.
14. Record of older generation past forty years, not spotless.
15. The old can learn from the young.
16. Enjoyment, not sinful: guiding principle for work and leisure; shed inhibitions.
17. Live in the present, not the past or the future.
18. Emphasis on the present: the shadow of the bomb; annihilation.
19. The young: question sanity of generation that bequeathed it.

The counter-argument: key words

1. The young do not seek responsibility: they evade it.
2. Too much money: they are spoilt.
3. Not interested in important questions; avoid involvement: e.g. major political issues, etc.
4. Interested only in themselves: *they* want material possessions (clothing, cars, etc.) without working for them.
5. The young should be grateful to older generation.
6. Older generation bequeathed peace and freedom which the young enjoy.
7. The older generation provided the young with good education, money to spend.
8. The older generation fought in two world wars; faced real problems. The young have had everything easy.
9. The young cling to passing fashions: clothes, pop music, etc.
10. Mass hysteria: a modern phenomenon.
11. Too much freedom, immorality; the young are shameless.
12. Appearance of many young people: disgusting: long hair; dirty, scruffy, lazy.
13. The older generation too soft and kind with the young; a tougher policy might work wonders.
14. The young are unadventurous; lack noble ideals; too clever by half.
15. Outlook for the world very bleak.

9 'Only stricter traffic laws can prevent accidents'

From the health point of view we are living in a marvellous age. We are immunised from birth against many of the most dangerous diseases. A large number of once fatal illnesses can now be cured by modern drugs and surgery. It is almost certain that one day remedies will be found for the most stubborn remaining diseases. The expectation of life has increased enormously. But though the possibility of living a long and happy life is greater than ever before, every day we witness the incredible slaughter of men, women and children on the roads. Man versus the motor-car! It is a never-ending battle which man is losing. Thousands of people the world over are killed or horribly mutilated each year and we are quietly sitting back and letting it happen.

It has been rightly said that when a man is sitting behind a steering wheel, his car becomes the extension of his personality. There is no doubt that the motor-car often brings out a man's very worst qualities. People who are normally quiet and pleasant may become unrecognisable when they are behind a steering-wheel. They swear, they are ill-mannered and aggressive, wilful as two-year-olds and utterly selfish. All their hidden frustrations, disappointments and jealousies seem to be brought to the surface by the act of driving.

The surprising thing is that society smiles so benignly on the motorist and seems to condone his behaviour. Everything is done for his convenience. Cities are allowed to become almost uninhabitable because of heavy traffic; towns are made ugly by huge car parks; the countryside is desecrated by road networks; and the mass annual slaughter becomes nothing more than a statistic, to be conveniently forgotten.

It is high time a world code were created to reduce this senseless waste of human life. With regard to driving, the laws of some countries are notoriously lax and even the strictest are not strict enough. A code which was universally accepted could only have a dramatically beneficial effect on the accident rate. Here are a few examples of some of the things that might be done. The driving test should be standardised and made far more difficult than it is; all drivers should be made to take a test every three years or so; the age at which young people are allowed to drive any vehicle should be raised to at least 21; all vehicles should be put through stringent annual tests for safety. Even the smallest amount of alcohol in the blood can impair a person's driving ability. Present drinking and driving laws (where they exist) should be made much stricter. Maximum and minimum speed limits should be imposed on all roads. Governments should lay down safety specifications for manufacturers, as has been done in the USA. All advertising stressing power and performance should be banned. These measures may sound inordinately harsh, but surely nothing should be considered as too severe if it results in reducing the annual toll of human life. After all, the world is for human beings, not motor-cars.

The argument: key words

1. Marvellous age from health point of view.
2. Immunisation from birth; cures: modern drugs, surgery.
3. Expectation of life increased.
4. But incredible slaughter on roads.
5. Man versus car: man, loser.
6. Thousands killed, maimed: we let it happen.
7. Car: extension of man's personality.
8. Brings out worst qualities: bad manners; aggression; selfishness.
9. Hidden frustrations, disappointments brought to the surface when driving.
10. Society seems to condone motorists' behaviour.
11. Everything done for the motorists' convenience: e.g. cities: heavy traffic; towns: car parks; the countryside: road networks.
12. Mass slaughter: a statistic; soon forgotten.
13. World code necessary.
14. Laws vary in countries: some lax; none too strict.
15. Strict world code would have beneficial effect.
16. E.g. more difficult driving test; test drivers every three years; raise age limit; annual safety test for vehicles; drinking and driving: stricter laws; maximum and minimum speed limits on all roads; government safety specifications: USA; curb advertising.
17. Measures not too harsh if lives saved; world for people, not cars.

The counter-argument: key words

1. Motor-cars are highly desirable for obvious reasons.
2. We should recognise this and adjust ourselves.
3. It's no use complaining and attacking the motorist – most of us are motorists.
4. It's nonsense to say countryside desecrated, cities spoilt, etc. All part of spread of communications.
5. The alternative is the isolated communities of the past.
6. Merely making stricter laws is not the best solution.
7. Will cost huge sums of money to enforce; perhaps not possible to enforce.
8. Best solution: provide better road facilities.
9. E.g. world-wide network of motorways; use of computers; universal adoption of multi-storey and underground car parks.
10. Possible introduction of small electric cars for cities in future; cars on rails, etc.
11. Laws are already strict enough. E.g. drinking and driving laws in Britain and other countries. Motorists – ordinary men and women – treated as potential criminals.
12. Motorists make possible huge industry, provide employment.
13. Motorists pay vast sums to exchequer: road tax, purchase tax, oil tax, etc.
14. Only a small proportion of money paid is used by governments to improve road conditions.
15. If all this money were used on roads, etc., the accident problem would be solved.

10 'Parents are too permissive with their children nowadays'

Few people would defend the Victorian attitude to children, but if you were a parent in those days, at least you knew where you stood: children were to be seen and not heard. Freud and company did away with all that and parents have been bewildered ever since. The child's happiness is all-important, the psychologists say, but what about the parents' happiness? Parents suffer constantly from fear and guilt while their children gaily romp about pulling the place apart. A good old-fashioned spanking is out of the question: no modern child-rearing manual would permit such barbarity. The trouble is you are not allowed even to shout. Who knows what deep psychological wounds you might inflict? The poor child may never recover from the dreadful traumatic experience. So it is that parents bend over backwards to avoid giving their children complexes which a hundred years ago hadn't even been heard of. Certainly a child needs love, and a lot of it. But the excessive permissiveness of modern parents is surely doing more harm than good.

Psychologists have succeeded in undermining parents' confidence in their own authority. And it hasn't taken children long to get wind of the fact. In addition to the great modern classics on child care, there are countless articles in magazines and newspapers. With so much unsolicited advice flying about, mum and dad just don't know what to do any more. In the end, they do nothing at all. So, from early childhood, the kids are in charge and parents lives are regulated according to the needs of their offspring. When the little dears develop into teenagers, they take complete control. Lax authority over the years makes adolescent rebellion against parents all the more violent. If the young people are going to have a party, for instance, parents are asked to leave the house. Their presence merely spoils the fun. What else can the poor parents do but obey?

Children are hardy creatures (far hardier than the psychologists would have us believe) and most of them survive the harmful influence of extreme permissiveness which is the normal condition in the modern household. But a great many do not. The spread of juvenile delinquency in our own age is largely due to parental laxity. Mother, believing that little Johnny can look after himself, is not at home when he returns from school, so little Johnny roams the streets. The dividing-line between permissiveness and sheer negligence is very fine indeed.

The psychologists have much to answer for. They should keep their mouths shut and let parents get on with the job. And if children are knocked about a little bit in the process, it may not really matter too much. At least this will help them to develop vigorous views of their own and give them something positive to react against. Perhaps there's some truth in the idea that children who've had a surfeit of happiness in their childhood emerge like stodgy puddings and fail to make a success of life.

The argument: key words

- 1 One can't defend Victorian attitude to children, but position clear then: children seen, not heard.
- 2 Freud and Co. have done away with this view.
- 3 Psychologists: child's happiness important. Parents'?
- 4 Parents: fear and guilt; spanking forbidden; barbarity.
- 5 Not even shouting: psychological wounds; traumatic experience.
- 6 Parents try to avoid giving complexes unknown 100 years ago.
- 7 Love, yes, but excessive permissiveness harmful.
- 8 Psychologists undermined parents' confidence in authority.
- 9 Children aware of this.
- 10 Bombarded with child-care books, articles, etc., parents don't know what to do; do nothing.
- 11 Regulate lives according to children's needs.
- 12 Lax authority: adolescent rebellion all the more violent.
- 13 E.g. parties: parents not wanted.
- 14 Children: hardy creatures; most survive permissiveness.
- 15 Many don't: juvenile delinquency; e.g. Johnny roams streets.
- 16 Dividing line, permissiveness and negligence very fine.
- 17 Psychologists to blame: leave parents alone.
- 18 If children knocked about a bit – not important.
- 19 Develop vigorous views, something positive to react against.
- 20 Surfeit of happiness: stodgy puddings?

The counter-argument: key words

- 1 If parents err today in bringing up children, they err on the right side.
- 2 There is no defence for Victorian harshness, hypocrisy, lack of understanding, barbarity.
- 3 We can only be grateful to Freud and Co.: an age of enlightenment.
- 4 Child-care manuals: sensible and practical; not authoritarian.
- 5 We know too much to be authoritarian these days.
- 6 Of course love is all important.
- 7 Love and care is not the same as permissiveness and negligence.
- 8 No one would defend parental laxity.
- 9 We are not concerned here with delinquent children, but with children from happy home backgrounds.
- 10 Psychological wounds can be very real.
- 11 E.g. can later lead to mental illness, etc.
- 12 Children today: healthy in body and mind; parents really care.
- 13 Develop more quickly than previous generation.
- 14 Soon gain independence from parents.
- 15 Grow up to be mature, responsible adults.

11 'Advertisers perform a useful service to the community'

Advertisers tend to think big and perhaps this is why they're always coming in for criticism. Their critics seem to resent them because they have a flair for self-promotion and because they have so much money to throw around. 'It's iniquitous,' they say, 'that this entirely unproductive industry (if we can call it that) should absorb millions of pounds each year. It only goes to show how much profit the big companies are making. Why don't they stop advertising and reduce the price of their goods? After all, it's the consumer who pays. . . .'

The poor old consumer! He'd have to pay a great deal more if advertising didn't create mass markets for products. It is precisely because of the heavy advertising that consumer goods are so cheap. But we get the wrong idea if we think the only purpose of advertising is to sell goods. Another equally important function is to *inform*. A great deal of the knowledge we have about household goods derives largely from the advertisements we read. Advertisements introduce us to new products or remind us of the existence of ones we already know about. Supposing you wanted to buy a washing-machine, it is more than likely you would obtain details regarding performance, price, etc., from an advertisement.

Lots of people pretend that they never read advertisements, but this claim may be seriously doubted. It is hardly possible *not* to read advertisements these days. And what fun they often are, too! Just think what a railway station or a newspaper would be like without advertisements. Would you enjoy gazing at a blank wall or reading railway bye-laws while waiting for a train? Would you like to read only closely-printed columns of news in your daily paper? A cheerful, witty advertisement makes such a difference to a drab wall or a newspaper full of the daily ration of calamities.

We must not forget, either, that advertising makes a positive contribution to our pockets. Newspapers, commercial radio and television companies could not subsist without this source of revenue. The fact that we pay so little for our daily paper, or can enjoy so many broadcast programmes is due entirely to the money spent by advertisers. Just think what a newspaper would cost if we had to pay its full price!

Another thing we mustn't forget is the 'small ads.' which are in virtually every newspaper and magazine. What a tremendously useful service they perform for the community! Just about anything can be accomplished through these columns. For instance, you can find a job, buy or sell a house, announce a birth, marriage or death in what used to be called the 'hatch, match and dispatch' columns; but by far the most fascinating section is the personal or 'agony' column. No other item in a newspaper provides such entertaining reading or offers such a deep insight into human nature. It's the best advertisement for advertising there is!

The argument: key words

1. Advertisers think big, always criticised.
2. Critics resent self-promotion, vast sums spent.
3. Arguments: unproductive 'industry', waste of money.
4. Stop advertising and reduce price of goods; consumer pays.
5. Advertising creates mass markets, therefore goods are cheap.
6. Purpose is not only to sell goods, but to inform.
7. We get information about household goods from advertisements.
8. E.g. washing-machine: details performance, price, etc.
9. Some claim they never read advertisements: doubtful.
10. Brighten up railway stations, newspapers.
11. Prefer blank wall, reading bye-laws, waiting for train?
12. Prefer newspapers full of calamities?
13. Contribution to our pockets.
14. Revenue for newspapers, commercial broadcasting.
15. Cost of newspaper if we paid full price?
16. Small ads: service to community.
17. Anything can be accomplished.
18. E.g. find job, buy, sell house, announce birth, marriage, death.
19. Personal column most fascinating: insight human nature.
20. Best advertisement for advertising.

The counter-argument: key words

1. It's frivolous to defend advertising because it provides cheerful reading matter.
2. Advertisements: an insidious form of brainwashing, using same techniques: slogans, catch-phrases, etc.
3. Creates demand for things we don't need.
4. Creates acquisitive society: demand for material things.
5. Advertising is offensive: appeals to baser instincts.
6. E.g. preys on our fears, our vanity, our greed, etc.
7. We are encouraged to buy insurance (fear); buy cosmetics (vanity); eat more than necessary (greed).
8. Advertisements unsightly: hoardings spoil countryside.
9. Cheapen the quality of life: most advertisements are in poor taste.
10. We have no choice: they are imposed on a captive audience: e.g. on television.
11. Shocking interruption of television programmes.
12. There's no doubt the big companies make too much profit.
13. E.g. 'free' gifts in soap packets; coupons in cigarette packets, etc.
14. Prices maintained high by artificial means.
15. Better and far more honest to sell in open competition on free market.
16. Good quality products don't need to be advertised.

12 'Pop stars certainly earn their money'

Pop stars today enjoy a style of living which was once the prerogative only of Royalty. Wherever they go, people turn out in their thousands to greet them. The crowds go wild trying to catch a brief glimpse of their smiling, colourfully-dressed idols. The stars are transported in their chauffeur-driven Rolls-Royces, private helicopters or executive aeroplanes. They are surrounded by a permanent entourage of managers, press-agents and bodyguards. Photographs of them appear regularly in the press and all their comings and goings are reported, for, like Royalty, pop stars are news. If they enjoy many of the privileges of Royalty, they certainly share many of the inconveniences as well. It is dangerous for them to make unscheduled appearances in public. They must be constantly shielded from the adoring crowds which idolise them. They are no longer private individuals, but public property. The financial rewards they receive for this sacrifice cannot be calculated, for their rates of pay are astronomical.

And why not? Society has always rewarded its top entertainers lavishly. The great days of Hollywood have become legendary: famous stars enjoyed fame, wealth and adulation on an unprecedented scale. By today's standards, the excesses of Hollywood do not seem quite so spectacular. A single gramophone record nowadays may earn much more in royalties than the films of the past ever did. The competition for the title 'Top of the Pops' is fierce, but the rewards are truly colossal.

It is only right that the stars should be paid in this way. Don't the top men in industry earn enormous salaries for the services they perform to their companies and their countries? Pop stars earn vast sums in foreign currency – often more than large industrial concerns – and the taxman can only be grateful for their massive annual contributions to the exchequer. So who would begrudge them their rewards?

It's all very well for people in humdrum jobs to moan about the successes and rewards of others. People who make envious remarks should remember that the most famous stars represent only the tip of the iceberg. For every famous star, there are hundreds of others struggling to earn a living. A man working in a steady job and looking forward to a pension at the end of it has no right to expect very high rewards. He has chosen security and peace of mind, so there will always be a limit to what he can earn. But a man who attempts to become a star is taking enormous risks. He knows at the outset that only a handful of competitors ever get to the very top. He knows that years of concentrated effort may be rewarded with complete failure. But he knows, too, that the rewards for success are very high indeed: they are the recompense for the huge risks involved and if he achieves them, he has certainly earned them. That's the essence of private enterprise.

The argument: key words

1. Pop stars: style of living once the prerogative only of Royalty.
2. Crowds to greet them everywhere.
3. Transported by Rolls-Royces, helicopters, executive aeroplanes.
4. Permanent entourage: managers, press agents, bodyguards.
5. Comings and goings recorded in press; pop stars are news.
6. Enjoy privileges of Royalty; share inconveniences.
7. No unscheduled appearances; must be shielded from adoring crowds.
8. Not private individuals; public property; astronomical rewards for this sacrifice.

9. Why not? Society always rewards top entertainers.
10. E.g. the legendary days of Hollywood; stars: fame, wealth, adulation.
11. Today even greater: one gramophone record may earn more than a film.
12. Fierce competition: Top of the Pops. Rewards colossal.

13. So they should be: compare top men in industry.
14. Foreign currency earned, often more than industrial concerns: massive contribution to exchequer.

15. People moan, envious of successes and rewards of others.
16. Most famous stars: tip of iceberg; hundreds struggling.
17. Compare man in steady job; no big rewards: security.
18. Would-be star: great risks; few reach the top; many fail.
19. Rewards for success: very high; the essence of private enterprise.

The counter-argument: key words

1. Rewards of pop stars make nonsense of sense of values in society.
2. Pop stars: a frivolous contribution to society; what they offer is wholly unnecessary.
3. Compare essential services: e.g. a surgeon saving people's lives: poor rewards by comparison.
4. Pop stars style of living outrageous: so much poverty in the world.

5. Big reputations are often artificially created.
6. Demand created by 'plugging' records.
7. 'Public image' of pop stars: the work of promoters.
8. Many lack real talent, even a knowledge of music; succeed in spite of this.

9. Pop stars exert undesirable influence in society.
10. E.g. mass hysteria among young people.
11. Create fashions: way of life, style of dress, etc., considered as ideal.
12. Pop music often associated with sub-culture: e.g. drug-taking and movements against the best interests of society.
13. Pop stars never use wealth and power to exert good influence.
14. Personal profit the sole motive.

13 'Vicious and dangerous sports should be banned by law'

When you think of the tremendous technological progress we have made, it's amazing how little we have developed in other respects. We may speak contemptuously of the poor old Romans because they relished the orgies of slaughter that went on in their arenas. We may despise them because they mistook these goings on for entertainment. We may forgive them condescendingly because they lived 2000 years ago and obviously knew no better. But are our feelings of superiority really justified? Are we any less blood-thirsty? Why do boxing matches, for instance, attract such universal interest? Don't the spectators who attend them hope they will see some violence? Human beings remain as bloodthirsty as ever they were. The only difference between ourselves and the Romans is that while they were honest enough to admit that they enjoyed watching hungry lions tearing people apart and eating them alive, we find all sorts of sophisticated arguments to defend sports which should have been banned long ago; sports which are quite as barbarous as, say, public hangings or bear-baiting.

It really is incredible that in this day and age we should still allow hunting or bull-fighting, that we should be prepared to sit back and watch two men batter each other to pulp in a boxing ring, that we should be relatively unmoved by the sight of one or a number of racing cars crashing and bursting into flames. Let us not deceive ourselves. Any talk of 'the sporting spirit' is sheer hypocrisy. People take part in violent sports because of the high rewards they bring. Spectators are willing to pay vast sums of money to see violence. A world heavyweight championship match, for instance, is front page news. Millions of people are disappointed if a big fight is over in two rounds instead of fifteen. They feel disappointment because they have been deprived of the exquisite pleasure of witnessing prolonged torture and violence.

Why should we ban violent sports if people enjoy them so much? You may well ask. The answer is simple: they are uncivilised. For centuries man has been trying to improve himself spiritually and emotionally – admittedly with little success. But at least we no longer tolerate the sight madmen cooped up in cages, or public floggings or any of the countless other barbaric practices which were common in the past. Prisons are no longer the grim forbidding places they used to be. Social welfare systems are in operation in many parts of the world. Big efforts are being made to distribute wealth fairly. These changes have come about not because human beings have suddenly and unaccountably improved, but because positive steps were taken to change the law. The law is the biggest instrument of social change that we have and it may exert great civilising influence. If we banned dangerous and violent sports, we would be moving one step further to improving mankind. We would recognise that violence is degrading and unworthy of human beings.

The argument: key words

1. Great technological progress; little in other respects.
2. We may despise the Romans: orgies of slaughter; entertainment 2000 years ago.
3. Are we less bloodthirsty?
4. E.g. boxing matches: spectators hope to see violence.
5. The Romans: honest enjoyment: lions eating people alive.
6. We have sophisticated arguments to defend barbaric sports.
7. We allow hunting, bull-fighting, boxing, car-racing.
8. 'Sporting spirit': sheer hypocrisy.
9. Participants take part for big rewards.
10. Spectators pay vast sums to see violence.
11. E.g. boxing matches: front page news.
12. Two rounds, not fifteen: disappointment.
13. Spectators deprived of pleasure: prolonged torture and violence.
14. Must ban violent sports: uncivilised.
15. Man: trying for centuries to improve spiritually, emotionally.
16. E.g. do not tolerate madmen in cages, public floggings, other barbaric practices.
17. Improvements: prisons, social welfare, fair distribution of wealth.
18. Positive steps to change society through the law.
19. Law: instrument of social change, civilising influence.
20. Ban sports: improve mankind; violence degrading.

The counter-argument: key words

1. Who is to decide which sports are violent and dangerous?
2. E.g. is football violent? What about unruly crowds?
3. Isn't deep-sea diving dangerous?
4. All the sports mentioned (boxing, etc.): thrilling to watch.
5. Sports like car-racing: not violent; explore limits of human skill and endurance.
6. Small element of violence does no harm: part of human nature.
7. Millions watch boxing matches: an emotional outlet.
8. Sports like this do good to community: help to get violence out of our systems.
9. Barbaric practices of the past (floggings, etc.): nothing to do with modern sports.
10. Sports have rarely been enforced or banned by law.
11. Sports evolved slowly and are refined: e.g. boxing: bare fists and today.
12. Elements of real danger removed: e.g. boxing matches are stopped; crashes on race tracks fairly rare.
13. There are elements of danger in all sports: that is their point.
14. Supreme tests of human skill: universal enjoyment.

14 'Transistor radios should be prohibited in public places'

We have all heard of the sort of person who drives fifty miles into the country, finds some perfectly delightful beauty spot beside a quiet lake and then spends the rest of the day cleaning his car. Compared with those terrible fiends, the litter-bugs and noise-makers, this innocent creature can only be an object of admiration. He interferes with no one's pleasure. Far from it: after all, cleanliness *is* said to be next to godliness. It is the noise-makers who invade the quietest corners of the earth that must surely win the prize for insensitivity. They announce their arrival with a flourish that would put the Royal Heralds to shame. Blaring music (never classical) seems to emanate mysteriously from their persons and their possessions. If you travel up the remotest reaches of the Amazon, surviving attacks by crocodiles and vicious piranha, don't be surprised if you hear cheering crowds and a football commentary shattering the peace of the jungle. It is only one of our friends with his little transistor radio. The transistor radio, that great wonder of modern technology, often no bigger than a matchbox, must surely be the most hideous and diabolic of all human inventions.

People are arrested, fined, imprisoned, deported, certified as insane or executed for being public nuisances. You can't loiter outside a shop for five minutes or sing the opening bars of *Figaro* in public without arousing the suspicion of every policeman in the neighbourhood. But you can walk on to a beach or into a park and let all hell loose with your little transistor and no one will turn a hair – no one in authority, that is. Most of the people around you will be writhing in agony, but what can they do about it? Have *you* ever tried asking the surly owner of a transistor to turn it off? This is what will happen if you do: you will either be punched on the nose for your impertinence, or completely ignored. After that you can be sure that the radio will be turned up louder than ever before.

Noise is one of the most unpleasant features of modern life. Who knows what it invisibly contributes to irritability and stress? Governments everywhere go to tremendous lengths to reduce noise. Traffic sounds are carefully measured in decibels; levels of tolerance are recorded and statistics produced to provide the basis for future legislation. Elaborate and expensive tests are conducted to find out our reactions to supersonic bangs. This is all very commendable, but surely the interest in our welfare is misplaced. People adjusted to the more obvious sources of noise ages ago. It is the less obvious sources that need attention. And the transistor radio is foremost among them. It is impossible to adjust to the transistor radio because the noise it produces is never the same: it can be anything from a brass band to a news commentary. Being inconsiderate is not a crime. But interfering with other people's pleasure certainly should be. It is ridiculous that the law should go on allowing this indecent assault on our ears.

The argument: key words

1. A person drives fifty miles: beauty spot beside lake; spends day cleaning car.
2. An innocent creature compared with litter-bugs, noise-makers; interferes with no one's pleasure.
3. Noise-makers invade quietest corners of earth: win prize for insensitivity.
4. Announce arrival noisily: blaring music emanates from them.
5. Go up Amazon, survive crocodiles, piranha: hear cheering crowds, football commentary; transistor.
6. One of the great wonders of technology: most hideous, diabolic of human inventions.
7. People fined, imprisoned, etc., as public nuisances.
8. If you loiter outside shop, sing in public, attract policemen in neighbourhood.
9. But walk on beach transistor blaring, no one in authority notices.
10. Most people writhing in agony, can't do anything about it.
11. Ever asked owner to turn off transistor?
12. Either punched on nose or ignored; radio louder than before.
13. Noise: one of the most unpleasant features of modern life.
14. Contributes invisibly to irritability, stress.
15. Governments try to reduce noise.
16. Traffic sounds measured, decibels; levels tolerance recorded; statistics, basis legislation; elaborate tests: supersonic bangs.
17. Interest misplaced; people adjusted long ago.
18. Less obvious source needs attention: transistor radio; people can't adjust; noise varies.
19. Should be a crime to interfere with others' pleasure.

The counter-argument: key words

1. You can't call music, etc., 'noise'! Can't compare it with cars, planes, etc.
2. Transistor owners perform a public service: share their pleasure.
3. Everyone enjoys sport, music, etc.
4. E.g. see how crowd collects round a transistor to hear a match commentary on beach.
5. Pleasant background music; no worse than music in restaurant.
6. Can't prohibit transistors legally, restrict human freedom.
7. Everyone has the right to listen to the radio.
8. If you prohibit transistors, you must ban other things too.
9. E.g. windows must be kept shut when radio is playing loudly.
10. Car radios must not play when a vehicle is stationary.
11. Open-air performances of music (brass bands, etc.) must be prohibited.
12. Open-air speeches, etc., must be prohibited.
13. Clearly this would be absurd legislation.
14. Who is trying to interfere with others' pleasure: those who want to prohibit transistors!

15 'The only thing people are interested in today is earning more money'

Once upon a time there lived a beautiful young woman and a handsome young man. They were very poor, but as they were deeply in love, they wanted to get married. The young people's parents shook their heads. 'You can't get married yet,' they said. 'Wait till you get a good job with good prospects.' So the young people waited until they found good jobs with good prospects and they were able to get married. They were still poor, of course. They didn't have a house to live in or any furniture, but that didn't matter. The young man had a good job with good prospects, so large organisations lent him the money he needed to buy a house, some furniture, all the latest electrical appliances and a car. The couple lived happily ever after paying off debts for the rest of their lives. And so ends another modern romantic fable.

We live in a materialistic society and are trained from our earliest years to be acquisitive. Our possessions, 'mine' and 'yours' are clearly labelled from early childhood. When we grow old enough to earn a living, it does not surprise us to discover that success is measured in terms of the money you earn. We spend the whole of our lives keeping up with our neighbours, the Joneses. If we buy a new television set, Jones is bound to buy a bigger and better one. If we buy a new car, we can be sure that Jones will go one better and get *two* new cars: one for his wife and one for himself. The most amusing thing about this game is that the Joneses and all the neighbours who are struggling frantically to keep up with them are spending borrowed money kindly provided, at a suitable rate of interest, of course, by friendly banks, insurance companies, etc.

It is not only in affluent societies that people are obsessed with the idea of making more money. Consumer goods are desirable everywhere and modern industry deliberately sets out to create new markets. Gone are the days when industrial goods were made to last forever. The wheels of industry must be kept turning. 'Built-in obsolescence' provides the means: goods are made to be discarded. Cars get tinnier and tinnier. You no sooner acquire this year's model than you are thinking about its replacement.

This materialistic outlook has seriously influenced education. Fewer and fewer young people these days acquire knowledge only for its own sake. Every course of studies must lead somewhere: i.e. to a bigger wage packet. The demand for skilled personnel far exceeds the supply and big companies compete with each other to recruit students before they have completed their studies. Tempting salaries and 'fringe benefits' are offered to them. Recruiting tactics of this kind have led to the 'brain drain', the process by which highly skilled people offer their services to the highest bidder. The wealthier nations deprive their poorer neighbours of their most able citizens. While Mammon is worshipped as never before, the rich get richer and the poor, poorer.

The argument: key words

1. Once upon a time: young woman, young man; poor, in love.
2. Parents objected to marriage: good job, good prospects first.
3. Young people complied: could get married.
4. Still poor: borrowed money for house, furniture, car, etc.
5. Lived happily ever after paying off debts; modern romantic fable.
6. We live in materialistic society; trained to be acquisitive.
7. 'Mine', 'yours' concepts from early childhood.
8. Success measured by money.
9. Keeping up with the Joneses: e.g. new TV; new car.
10. Jones and neighbours spending borrowed money, paying interest rates.
11. Not only affluent societies want more money; consumer goods desirable everywhere.
12. Modern industry creates new markets.
13. Wheels of industry: built-in obsolescence: e.g. cars.
14. Materialism influences education.
15. No knowledge for its own sake; purpose, more money.
16. Big firms compete; recruit students: big salaries, 'fringe benefits'.
17. Brain drain: services to highest bidder.
18. Wealthy nations deprive poorer neighbours of talented people.
19. Rich get richer; poor, poorer.

The counter-argument: key words

1. Interest in earning money not a modern phenomenon, but people not interested only in that.
2. Young people borrow money: a satisfactory arrangement: independent of parents, can start lives.
3. The argument proves nothing: only that living standards are better.
4. People interested in living decent lives consistent with human dignity.
5. Education is not money-orientated; it's skill-orientated; necessary because of modern technology.
6. Technology requires professionals, not amateurs.
7. Brain drain: skilled people are not always after more money but better work facilities.
8. A marked swing away from scientific studies has been noted: return to humanities; knowledge for its own sake.
9. Many young people not motivated by money: many reject materialistic values.
10. Many voluntary organisations (e.g. Peace Corps): idealistic, work without reward.
11. A marked reluctance to work long hours for money: desire to enjoy life.
12. Social welfare in many countries makes it unnecessary for people to struggle for money.
13. State provides: education, medical services, etc.
14. High taxes: a disincentive.

16 'Compulsory military service should be abolished in all countries'

Believe it or not, the Swiss were once a warlike people. There is still evidence of this. To this day, the guards at the Vatican are Swiss. But the Swiss discovered long ago that constant warfare brought them nothing but suffering and poverty. They adopted a policy of neutrality, and while the rest of the world seethed in turmoil, Switzerland, a country with hardly any natural resources, enjoyed peace and prosperity. The rest of the world is still not ready to accept this simple and obvious solution. Most countries not only maintain permanent armies but require all their young men to do a period of compulsory military service. Everybody has a lot to say about the desirability of peace, but no one does anything about it. An obvious thing to do would be to abolish conscription everywhere. This would be the first step towards universal peace.

Some countries, like Britain, have already abandoned peace-time conscription. Unfortunately, they haven't done so for idealistic reasons, but from a simple recognition of the fact that modern warfare is a highly professional business. In the old days, large armies were essential. There was strength in numbers; ordinary soldiers were cannon fodder. But in these days of inter-continental ballistic missiles, of push-button warfare and escalation, unskilled manpower has become redundant. In a mere two years or so, you can't hope to train conscripts in the requirements and conditions of modern warfare. So why bother? Leave it to the professionals!

There are also pressing personal reasons to abolish conscription. It is most unpleasant in times of peace for young men to grow up with the threat of military service looming over their heads. They are deprived of two of the best and most formative years of their lives. Their careers and studies are disrupted and sometimes the whole course of their lives is altered. They spend at least two years in the armed forces engaged in activities which do not provide them with any useful experience with regard to their future work. It can't even be argued that what they learn might prove valuable in a national emergency. When they leave the services, young men quickly forget all the unnecessary information about warfare which they were made to acquire. It is shocking to think that skilled and unskilled men are often nothing more than a source of cheap labour for the military.

Some people argue that military service 'does you good'. 'Two years in the army,' you hear people say, 'will knock some sense into him.' The opposite is usually the case. Anyone would resent being pushed about and bullied for two years, all in the name of 'discipline'. The military mind requires uniformity and conformity. People who do not quite fit into this brutal pattern suffer terribly and may even emerge with serious personality disorders. There are many wonderful ways of spending two years. Serving in the armed forces is not one of them!

The argument: key words

1. The Swiss: once a warlike people: Swiss guards, Vatican.
2. The Swiss discovered constant warfare: suffering, poverty.
3. Neutral policy: peace and prosperity.
4. Rest of world hasn't accepted this.
5. Most countries: permanent armies, compulsory military service.
6. First steps to peace: abolish conscription.

7. Some countries (e.g. Britain): abandoned conscription.
8. Not for idealistic reasons: recognition modern warfare is highly professional.
9. No strength in numbers; no need for cannon fodder.
10. Push-button warfare: unskilled manpower redundant.
11. Two years not enough to train conscripts. Leave it to professionals.

12. Personal reasons to abolish conscription.
13. Young men grow up with threat of two years' service; best, most formative years.
14. Careers, studies disrupted; even course of lives altered.
15. Useless experience: not valuable even in national emergency. Men forget what they learnt.
16. Skilled and unskilled men: source of cheap labour.

17. 'Does you good' argument: not true.
18. Young men pushed about, bullied: discipline. Uniformity and conformity.
19. Many suffer terribly; some: personality disorders.
20. Many wonderful ways of spending two years; armed forces not one of them.

The counter-argument: key words

1. Aim of peacetime conscription: national defence.
2. Insistence on conventional (not nuclear) warfare.
3. Therefore possibility of nuclear warfare is reduced.
4. Many examples of conventional warfare in recent times.

5. Two years in armed forces provide valuable experience of men; help a young man to grow up.
6. Valuable character training: stress on physical fitness, initiative, etc. A man can discover his abilities and limitations.
7. Helps with careers: many opportunities to study.
8. Helps qualified men to gain first experience in their careers (e.g. doctors, teachers, etc.).
9. Helps unskilled men to acquire skills (e.g. driving, vehicle maintenance, building, etc.).

10. Old-fashioned disciplinary measures not essential in modern armed services.
11. Great spirit of comradeship: morale high.
12. Many facilities available to servicemen for recreation, sports, etc.
13. Opportunities to travel overseas (e.g. UN peace-keeping forces, etc.).
14. Present-day defence arrangements are international: irresponsible for individual nations to opt out.

17 'Childhood is certainly not the happiest time of your life'

It's about time somebody exploded that hoary old myth about childhood being the happiest period of your life. Childhood may certainly be fairly happy, but it's greatest moments can't compare with the sheer joy of being an adult. Who ever asked a six-year-old for an opinion? Children don't have opinions, or if they do, nobody notices. Adults choose the clothes their children will wear, the books they will read and the friends they will play with. Mother and father are kindly but absolute dictators. This is an adult world and though children may be deeply loved, they have to be manipulated so as not to interfere too seriously with the lives of their elders and betters. The essential difference between manhood and childhood is the same as the difference between independence and subjection.

For all the nostalgic remarks you hear, which adult would honestly change places with a child? Think of the years at school: the years spent living in constant fear of examinations and school reports. Every movement you make, every thought you think is observed by some critical adult who may draw unflattering conclusions about your character. Think of the curfews, the martial law, the times you had to go to bed early, do as you were told, eat disgusting stuff that was supposed to be good for you. Remember how 'gentle' pressure was applied with remarks like 'if you don't do as I say, I'll . . .' and a dire warning would follow.

Even so, these are only part of a child's troubles. No matter how kind and loving adults may be, children often suffer from terrible, illogical fears which are the result of ignorance and an inability to understand the world around them. Nothing can equal the abject fear a child may feel in the dark, the absolute horror of childish nightmares. Adults can share their fears with other adults; children invariably face their fears alone. But the most painful part of childhood is the period when you begin to emerge from it: adolescence. Teenagers may rebel violently against parental authority, but this causes them great unhappiness. There is a complete lack of self-confidence during this time. Adolescents are over-conscious of their appearance and the impression they make on others. They feel shy, awkward and clumsy. Feelings are intense and hearts easily broken. Teenagers experience moments of tremendous elation or black despair. And through this turmoil, adults seem to be more hostile than ever.

What a relief it is to grow up. Suddenly you regain your balance; the world opens up before you. You are free to choose; you have your own place to live in and your own money to spend. You do not have to seek constant approval for everything you do. You are no longer teased, punished or ridiculed by heartless adults because you failed to come up to some theoretical standard. And if on occasion you are teased, you know how to deal with it. You can simply tell other adults to go to hell: you are one yourself.

The argument: key words

1. Childhood the happiest time of your life: a myth.
2. Happiest moments cannot compare with joy of being an adult.
3. Children don't have opinions; adults choose clothes, books, friends for them.
4. Parents: kindly but absolute dictators; children manipulated so as not to interfere with elders.
5. Difference between manhood and childhood: independence and subjection.

6. Nostalgic remarks, but who would change places?
7. Years of school: constant fear examinations, school reports.
8. Constant observation by critical adults; unflattering remarks.
9. Curfews; martial law; bed early; do as told; eat disgusting food.
10. 'Gentle' pressure; threats: 'if you don't do as I say . . .'.

11. Children suffer from illogical fears: ignorance of world around them.
12. E.g. abject fear of darkness; horror of nightmares; fears faced alone.
13. Most painful time: adolescence: rebellion against adult authority.
14. Lack of self-confidence; over-conscious appearance, impression on others.
15. Shy, awkward, clumsy. Intense feelings: elation or despair; adult world hostile.

16. Relief to grow up; regain balance.
17. Freedom to choose: where to live; money to spend.
18. Constant approval by adults not necessary.
19. Not subject to ridicule; if you are, you can deal with it.

The counter-argument: key words

1. What is the essence of happiness? Complete freedom from care.
2. Children have this: no responsibilities.
3. No social and economic pressures; no inhibitions.
4. They look at the world with fresh eyes; everything is new and unspoilt.
5. By comparison, adults are anxiety-ridden, tired, worried, etc.

6. Adolescent moments of intense happiness never recaptured.
7. Capacity for deep feeling; attachment to true values; idealism.
8. Willing to put up with discomforts, shortage of money, etc. Sheer joy of living.
9. Adults by comparison: bored, disillusioned, capacity to feel blunted.

10. Adult world is not the paradise it seems.
11. Adults also have to do as they are told; threatened by more senior adults (e.g. employers).
12. They are also under constant observation in their work; reports on them are filed in big firms.

13. It is significant that *most* adults think of their childhood as being most happy period.
14. One of the utopian dreams of mankind: to find the secret of eternal youth.

18 'Untidy people are not nice to know'

You don't have to be a genius to spot them. The men of the species are often uncombed; their ties never knotted squarely beneath their collars. The women of the species always manage to smear lipstick on their faces as well as their lips; in one hand they carry handbags which are stuffed full of accumulated rubbish; with the other, they drag a horde of neglected children behind them. With a sort of happy unconcern, both the male and female species litter railway stations, streets, parks, etc., with sweet wrappings, banana-skins, egg-shells and cast-off shoes. Who are they? That great untidy band of people that make up about three-quarters of the human race. An unending trail of rubbish pursues them wherever they go.

It is most unwise to call on them at their homes – particularly if they aren't expecting you. You are liable to find socks behind the refrigerator, marbles in the jam and egg-encrusted crockery. Newspapers litter the floor; ashtrays overflow; withered flowers go on withering in stale water. Writing-desks have become dumping grounds for piles of assorted, indescribable junk. And as for the bedrooms, well, it's best not to say. Avoid looking in their cars, too, because you are likely to find last year's lolly sticks, chewing-gum clinging to the carpets and a note saying 'Running In' on the rear window of a ten-year-old vehicle.

Yes, but what are they *really* like? Definitely not nice to know. They are invariably dirty, scruffy, forgetful, impatient, slovenly, slothful, unpunctual, inconsiderate, rude, irritable and (if they're driving a car) positively dangerous. Untidiness and these delightful qualities always seem to go together, or shall we say that untidiness *breeds* these qualities. It's hardly surprising. If you are getting dressed and can only find one sock, you can only end up being irritable and scruffy. If after a visit to a lovely beauty spot you think that other people will enjoy the sight of *your* orange peel, you can only be inconsiderate and slovenly. If you can't find an important letter because you stuck it between the pages of a book and then returned the book to the library, you can only be forgetful. If you live in perpetual, self-imposed squalor, you must be slothful – otherwise you'd do something about it.

What a delightful minority tidy people are by comparison! They seem to have a monopoly of the best human qualities. They are clean, neat, patient, hard-working, punctual, considerate and polite. All these gifts are reflected in their homes, their gardens, their work, their personal appearance. They are radiant, welcoming people whom you long to meet, whose esteem you really value. The crux of the matter is that tidy people are kind and generous, while untidy people are mean and selfish. The best proof of this is that tidy people, acting on the highest, selfless motives, invariably marry untidy ones. What happens after that is another story!

The argument: key words

- 1 Easy to spot: men of species, uncombed, untidy.
- 2 Women: smeared lipstick; handbags stuffed with rubbish; horde of neglected children.
- 3 Male and female species: leave litter at railway stations, streets, etc.
- 4 Who are they? Untidy people; three-quarters human race; trail of rubbish pursues them.

- 5 Unwise to call at their homes – especially if not expected.
- 6 Might find: e.g. socks behind refrigerator; marbles in jam.
- 7 Newspapers on floor; overflowing ashtrays; withered flowers withering.
- 8 Desks: dumping grounds for junk; bedrooms: best not to say.
- 9 Cars: old lolly sticks; chewing gum, carpets; 'Running In' – ten-year-old vehicle.

- 10 Not nice people to know: irritable, inconsiderate, forgetful, slothful, etc.
- 11 Untidiness breeds these qualities; hardly surprising.
- 12 E.g. Irritable if you can only find one sock.
- 13 Inconsiderate if you leave litter at beauty spots.
- 14 Forgetful: can't find letter; stuck in book returned to library.
- 15 Slothful: live in self-imposed squalor, do nothing about it.

- 16 Tidy people delightful by comparison; monopoly of best qualities.
- 17 Clean, neat, patient, etc., reflected in homes, gardens, personal appearance.
- 18 Radiant, welcoming people; long to meet them; value their esteem.
- 19 Tidy people: kind, generous. Untidy ones: mean, selfish.
- 20 Tidy people usually marry untidy ones: another story.

The counter-argument: key words

- 1 People obsessed with tidiness are not quite human.
- 2 Possess very bad qualities: nagging; mean; jealous; spoil-sports; old-fashioned; narrow-minded; prudish; self-satisfied prigs.
- 3 E.g. house-proud housewife: family not allowed even to walk on floors! Houses like museums.
- 4 Husbands: tidy desks on which work is never done; tidy shelves of books never read.

- 5 Tidy people can't enjoy life; don't know how to live.
- 6 Slaves of material things. Hygienic lives: always polishing floors, cleaning cars, etc.
- 7 Their children are insufferable: always dressed in best suits; not allowed to play.

- 8 Tidy people: lack ideas, are uncreative.
- 9 Never have time to create anything; always pursued by things.
- 10 Hypocrites: interested only in outward appearances.

- 11 Unfriendly people: their way of life doesn't encourage friendship.
- 12 Usually introvert: always thinking about themselves and their possessions.
- 13 Very often depressed, unhappy; mental hospitals are full of tidy people.

19 'The only way to travel is on foot'

The past ages of man have all been carefully labelled by anthropologists. Descriptions like 'Palaeolithic Man', 'Neolithic Man', etc., neatly sum up whole periods. When the time comes for anthropologists to turn their attention to the twentieth century, they will surely choose the label 'Legless Man'. Histories of the time will go something like this: 'In the twentieth century, people forgot how to use their legs. Men and women moved about in cars, buses and trains from a very early age. There were lifts and escalators in all large buildings to prevent people from walking. This situation was forced upon earth-dwellers of that time because of their extraordinary way of life. In those days, people thought nothing of travelling hundreds of miles each day. But the surprising thing is that they didn't use their legs even when they went on holiday. They built cable railways, ski-lifts and roads to the top of every huge mountain. All the beauty spots on earth were marred by the presence of large car parks.'

The future history books might also record that we were deprived of the use of our eyes. In our hurry to get from one place to another, we failed to see anything on the way. Air travel gives you a bird's-eye view of the world – or even less if the wing of the aircraft happens to get in your way. When you travel by car or train a blurred image of the countryside constantly smears the windows. Car drivers, in particular, are forever obsessed with the urge to go *on* and *on*: they never want to stop. Is it the lure of the great motorways, or what? And as for sea travel, it hardly deserves mention. It is perfectly summed up in the words of the old song: 'I joined the navy to see the world, and what did I see? I saw the sea.' The typical twentieth-century traveller is the man who always says 'I've been there.' You mention the remotest, most evocative place-names in the world like El Dorado, Kabul, Irkutsk and someone is bound to say 'I've been there' – meaning, 'I drove through it at 100 miles an hour on the way to somewhere else.'

When you travel at high speeds, the present means nothing: you live mainly in the future because you spend most of your time looking forward to arriving at some other place. But actual arrival, when it is achieved, is meaningless. You want to move on again. By travelling like this, you suspend all experience; the present ceases to be a reality: you might just as well be dead. The traveller on foot, on the other hand, lives constantly in the present. For him travelling and arriving are one and the same thing: he arrives somewhere with every step he makes. He experiences the present moment with his eyes, his ears and the whole of his body. At the end of his journey he feels a delicious physical weariness. He knows that sound, satisfying sleep will be his: the just reward of all true travellers.

The argument: key words

1. Past ages carefully labelled by anthropologists: Palaeolithic Man, Neolithic Man, etc.
2. Twentieth century: anthropologists' label: 'Legless Man'.
3. A history of this time might sound like this:
4. Twentieth century: people forgot use of legs; used cars, buses, trains from early age.
5. Lifts, escalators in all buildings prevented them from walking.
6. Situation forced upon earth-dwellers: way of life; travelled long distances.
7. Even on holiday: cable railways, ski-lifts, roads to tops of mountains.
8. Don't use our eyes any more: hurry to get from place to place.
9. Air travel: a bird's-eye view of the world, or less.
10. Car and train: a blurred image of the countryside.
11. Car drivers: urge to go on and on without stopping; motorways to blame?
12. Sea travel: summed up in old song: 'I joined the navy . . .'
13. Typical twentieth-century traveller: 'I've been there'. El Dorado, Kabul, Irkutsk: through at 100 miles an hour.
14. When travelling at high speeds present means nothing: life in future.
15. Actual arrival is meaningless; want to move on.
16. Suspend all experience; present no longer a reality; might as well be dead.
17. Traveller on foot: lives constantly in present.
18. Travelling and arriving: the same thing; arrives with every step.
19. Experiences present moment: ears, eyes, whole body.
20. End of journey: weariness, satisfying sleep: just reward.

The counter-argument: key words

1. Travelling at high speeds is a means not an end.
2. But it is also a pleasure in itself.
3. E.g. drivers experience great thrill, satisfaction, travelling long distances.
4. Air travel: exciting; unusual view of world.
5. Sea travel: a holiday in itself; modern ships are floating cities.
6. Approach to travel in twentieth century: practical and labour-saving.
7. Foolish to climb a mountain when there's a railway or road up it.
8. Travelling on foot: exhausting: you get nowhere fast.
9. If we depended on our legs, we would be isolated from each other, as in the past.
10. Modern means of communication make the world a small place.
11. It's now possible to see many countries, meet people of all nationalities.
12. Man uses his intelligence to extend his abilities: e.g. computers *extend*, not replace the use of our brains.
13. Modern means of travel extend, not replace the use of our legs.
14. Future anthropologists (and others) will have much to be grateful for.

20 'Examinations exert a pernicious influence on education'

We might marvel at the progress made in every field of study, but the methods of testing a person's knowledge and ability remain as primitive as ever they were. It really is extraordinary that after all these years, educationists have still failed to devise anything more efficient and reliable than examinations. For all the pious claim that examinations test what you know, it is common knowledge that they more often do the exact opposite. They may be a good means of testing memory, or the knack of working rapidly under extreme pressure, but they can tell you nothing about a person's true ability and aptitude.

As anxiety-makers, examinations are second to none. That is because so much depends on them. They are the mark of success or failure in our society. Your whole future may be decided in one fateful day. It doesn't matter that you weren't feeling very well, or that your mother died. Little things like that don't count: the exam goes on. No one can give of his best when he is in mortal terror, or after a sleepless night, yet this is precisely what the examination system expects him to do. The moment a child begins school, he enters a world of vicious competition where success and failure are clearly defined and measured. Can we wonder at the increasing number of 'drop-outs': young people who are written off as utter failures before they have even embarked on a career? Can we be surprised at the suicide rate among students?

A good education should, among other things, train you to think for yourself. The examination system does anything but that. What has to be learnt is rigidly laid down by a syllabus, so the student is encouraged to memorise. Examinations do not motivate a student to read widely, but to restrict his reading; they do not enable him to seek more and more knowledge, but induce cramming. They lower the standards of teaching, for they deprive the teacher of all freedom. Teachers themselves are often judged by examination results and instead of teaching their subjects, they are reduced to training their students in exam techniques which they despise. The most successful candidates are not always the best educated; they are the best trained in the technique of working under duress.

The results on which so much depends are often nothing more than a subjective assessment by some anonymous examiner. Examiners are only human. They get tired and hungry; they make mistakes. Yet they have to mark stacks of hastily scrawled scripts in a limited amount of time. They work under the same sort of pressure as the candidates. And their word carries weight. After a judge's decision you have the right of appeal, but not after an examiner's. There must surely be many simpler and more effective ways of assessing a person's true abilities. Is it cynical to suggest that examinations are merely a profitable business for the institutions that run them? This is what it boils down to in the last analysis. The best comment on the system is this illiterate message recently scrawled on a wall: 'I were a teenage drop-out and now I are a teenage millionaire.'

The argument: key words

1. Great progress in many fields, but exams: a primitive method of testing knowledge and ability.
2. Educationists haven't devised anything more efficient, reliable.
3. Exams should test what you know; often do the opposite.
4. Test of memory, working under pressure; not ability, aptitude.
5. Exams cause anxiety: mark of success or failure; future decided by them.
6. Personal factors (e.g. health, mother's death) immaterial.
7. Cannot give of your best if in terror or after sleepless night.
8. School: vicious competition: success, failure clearly defined, measured.
9. Increasing number of 'drop-outs', suicides.
10. Education should train you to think for yourself; exam system doesn't.
11. Exams encourage memorisation; restrict reading; induce cramming.
12. They lower teaching standards; teacher: no freedom.
13. Teachers often judged by exam results; therefore teach exam techniques.
14. Most successful candidates not best educated; best trained in techniques.
15. Results: subjective assessment by examiner.
16. Examiners human: tired, hungry, make mistakes, work under pressure.
17. After judge's decision, right of appeal; not after examiner's.
18. There must be more effective ways of assessing ability.
19. Exams merely a profitable business?

The counter-argument: key words

1. Exams are a well-tried system: many advantages.
2. They offer the best *quick* way of assessing a candidate.
3. Their reliability has been proved again and again.
4. They are marked anonymously: therefore reliable.
5. Not possible to do well relying merely on memory and exam techniques.
6. They are often not the only way of assessing a candidate: used in connection with teachers' assessments.
7. Exams are constantly being improved.
8. There are complex checking systems used by examiners to ensure fair results.
9. There is a lot of research into objective testing techniques to eliminate human error.
10. Computers are already widely used to mark specially devised tests.
11. Pernicious aspects of system (cramming, etc.) are not the fault of examinations, but of the teacher.
12. Teachers cram weak pupils to push them through; able pupils don't need cramming.
13. Teachers want examinations: they provide a clear objective.
14. The exam system may not be perfect, but it's the best we have; it may be painful, but so are many things in life.

21 'Books, plays and films should be censored'

Let us suppose that you are in the position of a parent. Would you allow your children to read any book they wanted to without first checking its contents? Would you take your children to see any film without first finding out whether it is suitable for them? If your answer to these questions is 'yes', then you are either extremely permissive, or just plain irresponsible. If your answer is 'no', then you are exercising your right as a parent to protect your children from what you consider to be undesirable influences. In other words, by acting as a censor yourself, you are admitting that there is a strong case for censorship.

Now, of course, you will say that it is one thing to exercise censorship where children are concerned and quite another to do the same for adults. Children need protection and it is the parents' responsibility to provide it. But what about adults? Aren't they old enough to decide what is good for them? The answer is that many adults are, but don't make the mistake of thinking that all adults are like yourself. Censorship is for the good of society *as a whole*. Highly civilised people might find it possible to live amicably together without laws of any kind: they would just rely on good sense to solve their problems. But imagine what chaos there would be if we lived in a society without laws! Like the law, censorship contributes to the common good.

Some people think that it is disgraceful that a censor should interfere with works of art. Who is this person, they say, to ban this great book or cut that great film? No one can set himself up as a superior being. But we must remember two things. Firstly, where genuine works of art are concerned, modern censors are extremely liberal in their views – often far more liberal than a large section of the public. Artistic merit is something which censors clearly recognise. And secondly, we must bear in mind that the great proportion of books, plays and films which come before the censor are very far from being 'works of art'.

When discussing censorship, therefore, we should not confine our attention to great masterpieces, but should consider the vast numbers of publications and films which make up the bulk of the entertainment industry. When censorship laws are relaxed, unscrupulous people are given a licence to produce virtually anything in the name of 'art'. There is an increasing tendency to equate 'artistic' with 'pornographic'. The vast market for pornography would rapidly be exploited. One of the great things that censorship does is to prevent certain people from making fat profits by corrupting the minds of others. To argue in favour of absolute freedom is to argue in favour of anarchy. Society would really be the poorer if it deprived itself of the wise counsel and the restraining influence which a censor provides.

The argument: key words

1. Put yourself in position of parent: let children read any book, see any film?
2. Yes: permissive or irresponsible.
3. No: exercising a parent's right to protect children.
4. Acting as censor, therefore admitting a case for censorship.
5. Children need protection, different from adults?
6. Not all adults mature enough to decide what's good for them.
7. Censorship good for society as a whole.
8. Civilised people might do without laws, but not whole society.
9. Censorship is like the law: for the common good.
10. People think a censor must not interfere with works of art.
11. But censors are extremely liberal: recognise merit.
12. Majority of books, plays, films are not works of art.
13. We must not confine attention to masterpieces.
14. Numerous publications, films: bulk of entertainment industry.
15. Unscrupulous people: produce anything in the name of art; exploit vast pornography market.
16. Tendency to equate 'artistic' and 'pornographic'.
17. Censorship prevents profits from corrupting minds of others.
18. Absolute freedom equals anarchy.
19. Censor: wise counsel, restraining influence.

The counter-argument: key words

1. Parents protecting children: not relevant to the argument.
2. Books, plays, films should be considered under common law: not under special censorship code.
3. Dangerous to admit the principle of censorship.
4. Censorship limits and controls the way people feel and think.
5. What it leads to: e.g. in totalitarian countries: outrageous decisions.
6. Not consistent with the ideals of democracy.
7. Who shall be censor? What qualifications for this super-being?
8. Many idiotic decisions by 'protectors of public' from Bowdler onwards.
9. Censorship does not prevent pornography; market always exists and is exploited whether there is a censor or not.
10. Any publication or film offensive to decency would still be liable to prosecution without censorship.
11. Censors do not distinguish between 'works of art' and others.
12. They cut and ban indiscriminately: make subjective decisions.
13. Banning books, etc., has the effect of drawing attention to them and vastly increasing sales.
14. This can never happen in a society free from censorship. E.g. Denmark.

22 'People should be rewarded according to ability, not according to age and experience'

Young men and women today are finding it more and more necessary to protest against what is known as the 'Establishment': that is, the people who wield power in our society. Clashes with the authorities are reported almost daily in the press. The tension that exists between old and young could certainly be lessened if some of the most obvious causes were removed. In particular, the Establishment should adopt different attitudes to work and the rewards it brings. Today's young people are ambitious. Many are equipped with fine educations and are understandably impatient to succeed as quickly as possible. They want to be able to have their share of the good things in life while they are still young enough to enjoy them. The Establishment, however, has traditionally believed that people should be rewarded according to their age and experience. Ability counts for less. As the Establishment controls the purse-strings, its views are inevitably imposed on society. Employers pay the smallest sum consistent with keeping you in a job. You join the hierarchy and take your place in the queue. If you are young, you go to the very end of the queue and stay there no matter how brilliant you are. *What* you know is much less important than *whom* you know and how old you are. If you are able, your abilities will be acknowledged and rewarded in due course – that is, after twenty or thirty years have passed. By that time you will be considered old enough to join the Establishment and you will be expected to adopt its ideals. God help you if you don't.

There seems to be a gigantic conspiracy against young people. While on the one hand society provides them with better educational facilities, on the other it does its best to exclude them from the jobs that really matter. There are exceptions, of course. Some young people do manage to break through the barrier despite the restrictions, but the great majority have to wait patiently for years before they can really give full rein to their abilities. This means that, in most fields, the views of young people are never heard because there is no one to represent them. All important decisions about how society is to be run are made by people who are too old to remember what it was like to be young. President Kennedy was one of the notable exceptions. One of the most tragic aspects of his assassination is that mankind was deprived of a youthful leader.

Resentment is the cause of a great deal of bitterness. The young resent the old because they feel deprived of the good things life has to offer. The old resent the young because they are afraid of losing what they have. A man of fifty or so might say, 'Why should a young rascal straight out of school earn more than I do?' But if the young rascal is more able, more determined, harder-working than his middle-aged critic, why shouldn't he? Employers should recognise ability and reward it justly. This would remove one of the biggest causes of friction between old and young and ultimately it would lead to a better society.

The argument: key words

- 1 Young people frequently protest against the Establishment.
- 2 Tension could be lessened if causes were removed.
- 3 Big difference in attitude to work and rewards.
- 4 The young today: ambitious, well-educated, eager to succeed.
- 5 The Establishment believes in rewarding according to age and experience; ability secondary.
- 6 Controls purse-strings: pays the smallest possible sums.
- 7 The young join hierarchy at the end of the queue; *what* you know less important than *whom* you know.
- 8 Rewards come after twenty or thirty years.
- 9 By that time, old enough to join Establishment, adopt its ideals.
- 10 Big conspiracy against the young.
- 11 Society provides a good education, withholds important jobs.
- 12 Very few young people break through barrier.
- 13 Views of the young not represented; the old make decisions. Kennedy a notable exception.
- 14 Resentment causes bitterness.
- 15 The young resent the old: feel deprived of the good things in life.
- 16 The old resent the young: afraid of losing what they have.
- 17 E.g. a man of fifty resents a young man earning more.
- 18 Society must recognise ability and reward accordingly.
- 19 Cause of friction between the old and young would be removed.

The counter-argument: key words

- 1 There is a hierarchy, but young people rise up scale more quickly than ever before.
- 2 Young people mature more quickly, assume responsibilities.
- 3 Many young people in teens, early twenties: great success.
- 4 Many others successful by late twenties, early thirties.
- 5 Attitudes to work not a cause of friction between Establishment and young.
- 6 Clashes due to other causes: different sets of values.
- 7 In a free society, people are rewarded according to many factors, not just ability, age, etc. E.g. enterprise, initiative, etc.
- 8 Young people are free to compete on equal terms in democratic society.
- 9 Big organisations (e.g. large firms, civil service) could not function without hierarchy.
- 10 Big organisations are quick to spot and acknowledge ability.
- 11 It's only fair that a young man should receive smaller rewards.
- 12 Experience is a valuable commodity, hard to obtain.
- 13 Older people have great responsibilities: young families, ageing parents.
- 14 In society, everyone gets what he deserves.

23 'The tourist trade contributes absolutely nothing to increasing understanding between nations'

The tourist trade is booming. With all this coming and going, you'd expect greater understanding to develop between the nations of the world. Not a bit of it! Superb systems of communication by air, sea and land make it possible for us to visit each other's countries at a moderate cost. What was once the 'grand tour', reserved for only the very rich, is now within everybody's grasp. The package tour and chartered flights are not to be sneered at. Modern travellers enjoy a level of comfort which the lords and ladies on grand tours in the old days couldn't have dreamed of. But what's the sense of this mass exchange of populations if the nations of the world remain basically ignorant of each other?

Many tourist organisations are directly responsible for this state of affairs. They deliberately set out to protect their clients from too much contact with the local population. The modern tourist leads a cosseted, sheltered life. He lives at international hotels, where he eats his international food and sips his international drink while he gazes at the natives from a distance. Conducted tours to places of interest are carefully censored. The tourist is allowed to see only what the organisers want him to see and no more. A strict schedule makes it impossible for the tourist to wander off on his own; and anyway, language is always a barrier, so he is only too happy to be protected in this way. At its very worst, this leads to a new and hideous kind of colonisation. The summer quarters of the inhabitants of the *cité universitaire:* are temporarily re-established on the island of Corfu. Blackpool is recreated at Torremolinos where the traveller goes not to eat paella, but fish and chips.

The sad thing about this situation is that it leads to the persistence of national stereotypes. We don't see the people of other nations as they really are, but as we have been brought up to believe they are. You can test this for yourself. Take five nationalities, say, French, German, English, American and Italian. Now in your mind, match them with these five adjectives: musical, amorous, cold, pedantic, naïve. Far from providing us with any insight into the national characteristics of the peoples just mentioned, these adjectives actually act as barriers. So when you set out on your travels, the only characteristics you notice are those which confirm your preconceptions. You come away with the highly unoriginal and inaccurate impression that, say, 'Anglo-saxons are hypocrites' or that 'Latin peoples shout a lot'. You only have to make a few foreign friends to understand how absurd and harmful national stereotypes are. But how can you make foreign friends when the tourist trade does its best to prevent you?

Carried to an extreme, stereotypes can be positively dangerous. Wild generalisations stir up racial hatred and blind us to the basic fact – how trite it sounds! – that all people are human. We are all similar to each other and at the same time all unique.

The argument: key words

1. Considerable tourist traffic, but no greater understanding between nations.
2. Superb system of communication: air, sea, land; moderate cost.
3. Grand tour: for very rich. Now: package tour: high level comfort.
4. What's the sense, if ignorant of each other?

5. Tourist organisations responsible: protect clients from local people.
6. Modern tourist: a sheltered life; international hotels, food, etc.
7. Local sight-seeing censored by organisers.
8. Tourists happy to be protected.
9. New and hideous colonisation: e.g. *cité universitaire:* Corfu; Blackpool: Torremolinos.

10. This leads to persistence of national stereotypes.
11. See others not as they are, but as we have been taught to believe they are.
12. Test for yourself: match French, German, English, American, Italian with: musical, amorous, cold, pedantic, naïve.
13. Adjectives: no insight into characteristics, but barriers.
14. When travelling you notice characteristics which confirm preconceptions.
15. E.g. Anglo-saxons: hypocrites; Latin peoples: noisy.
16. Foreign friends make you understand stereotypes absurd, harmful.
17. Tourist trade prevents you making foreign friends.

18. Stereotypes: dangerous, can stir up racial hatred.
19. All people human; all similar; all unique.

The counter-argument: key words

1. Stereotypes: nothing to do with tourist trade.
2. Idea of stereotypes only a party joke anyway.
3. Tourism contributes enormously to international understanding.
4. Pre-war days hardly anyone travelled; today hardly anyone doesn't.
5. This in itself cannot fail to lead to understanding.
6. E.g. consider the way nations influence each other: fashions, eating habits, etc.
7. Many examples of 'national' fashions becoming world fashions.

8. World today: a small place; barriers breaking down everywhere.
9. E.g. European Economic Community; United Nations, etc.
10. Increasing tendency to identify with larger groups.
11. Great interest in language learning.

12. People who are 'protected' at international hotels are old and rich.
13. The young are more impressionable, not so 'protected'.
14. People are eager to get to know each other; curious about different way of life.

24 'Only a madman would choose to live in a large modern city'

'Avoid the rush-hour' must be the slogan of large cities the world over. If it is, it's a slogan no one takes the least notice of. Twice a day, with predictable regularity, the pot boils over. Wherever you look it's people, people, people. The trains which leave or arrive every few minutes are packed: an endless procession of human sardine tins. The streets are so crowded, there is hardly room to move on the pavements. The queues for buses reach staggering proportions. It takes ages for a bus to get to you because the traffic on the roads has virtually come to a standstill. Even when a bus does at last arrive, it's so full, it can't take any more passengers. This whole crazy system of commuting stretches man's resources to the utmost. The smallest unforeseen event can bring about conditions of utter chaos. A power-cut, for instance, an exceptionally heavy snowfall or a minor derailment must always make city-dwellers realise how precarious the balance is. The extraordinary thing is not that people put up with these conditions, but that they actually choose them in preference to anything else.

Large modern cities are too big to control. They impose their own living conditions on the people who inhabit them. City-dwellers are obliged by their environment to adopt a wholly unnatural way of life. They lose touch with the land and rhythm of nature. It is possible to live such an air-conditioned existence in a large city that you are barely conscious of the seasons. A few flowers in a public park (if you have the time to visit it) may remind you that it is spring or summer. A few leaves clinging to the pavement may remind you that it is autumn. Beyond that, what is going on in nature seems totally irrelevant. All the simple, good things of life like sunshine and fresh air are at a premium. Tall buildings blot out the sun. Traffic fumes pollute the atmosphere. Even the distinction between day and night is lost. The flow of traffic goes on unceasingly and the noise never stops.

The funny thing about it all is that you pay dearly for the 'privilege' of living in a city. The demand for accommodation is so great that it is often impossible for ordinary people to buy a house of their own. Exorbitant rents must be paid for tiny flats which even country hens would disdain to live in. Accommodation apart, the cost of living is very high. Just about everything you buy is likely to be more expensive than it would be in the country.

In addition to all this, city-dwellers live under constant threat. The crime rate in most cities is very high. Houses are burgled with alarming frequency. Cities breed crime and violence and are full of places you would be afraid to visit at night. If you think about it, they're not really fit to live in at all. Can anyone really doubt that the country is what man was born for and where he truly belongs?

The argument: key words

1. 'Avoid rush-hour': slogan of every large city; no one does.
2. Happens twice a day.
3. Trains packed; streets crowded; bus queues; traffic jams; buses full.
4. Commuting stretches man's resources.
5. Unforeseen events (e.g. power-cut, heavy snowfall): chaos.
6. People actually choose such conditions.
7. Large modern cities too big to control.
8. Impose their own living conditions on people.
9. City-dwellers: unnatural way of life.
10. Lose touch with land, rhythms of nature.
11. Air-conditioned existence: barely conscious of seasons: flowers: spring; leaves: autumn; nature irrelevant.
12. Simple good things (e.g. sunlight, fresh air) at a premium.
13. Distinction day, night is lost; always noise, traffic.
14. Expensive 'privilege'.
15. Accommodation: house of your own impossible; rents high.
16. Cost of living in general high.
17. Lack of security: cities breed crime and violence; houses often burgled.
18. Cities not fit to live in; man born for country.

The counter-argument: key words

1. If proposition is true, then there are millions of madmen.
2. Most people love cities: proof: man is fleeing from countryside.
3. Modern man too sophisticated for simple country pleasures.
4. It's enough to visit countryside at week-ends.
5. Objections to city living are unconvincing:
6. Commuting does not really affect those who *live* in cities; a small inconvenience only.
7. Noise, traffic, etc., hardly noticeable; people easily adapt.
8. Very small minority of city-dwellers ever involved in crime, violence.
9. Many reasons why city life is preferable:
10. Good to be near one's friends; never cut off by weather conditions.
11. Life is never dull; always something to do.
12. Cities offer high concentration of good things in life: big stores, restaurants, theatres, cinemas, galleries, etc.
13. Services are always better: better schools, more amenities (e.g. swimming-pools, etc.).
14. More chances of employment; greater range of jobs; more opportunity to succeed in life.

25 'Equality of opportunity in the twentieth century has not destroyed the class system'

These days we hear a lot of nonsense about the 'great classless society'. The idea that the twentieth century is the age of the common man has become one of the great clichés of our time. The same old arguments are put forward in evidence. Here are some of them: monarchy as a system of government has been completely descredited. The monarchies that survive have been deprived of all political power. Inherited wealth has been savagely reduced by taxation and, in time, the great fortunes will disappear altogether. In a number of countries the victory has been complete. The people rule; the great millenium has become a political reality. But has it? Close examination doesn't bear out the claim.

It is a fallacy to suppose that all men are equal and that society will be levelled out if you provide everybody with the same educational opportunities. (It is debatable whether you can ever provide everyone with the same educational opportunities, but that is another question.) The fact is that nature dispenses brains and ability with a total disregard for the principle of equality. The old rules of the jungle, 'survival of the fittest', and 'might is right' are still with us. The spread of education has destroyed the old class system and created a new one. Rewards are based on merit. For 'aristocracy' read 'meritocracy'; in other respects, society remains unaltered: the class system is rigidly maintained.

Genuine ability, animal cunning, skill, the knack of seizing opportunities, all bring material rewards. And what is the first thing people do when they become rich? They use their wealth to secure the best possible opportunities for their children, to give them 'a good start in life'. For all the lip-service we pay to the idea of equality, we do not consider this wrong in the western world. Private schools which offer unfair advantages over state schools are not banned because one of the principles in a democracy is that people should be free to choose how they will educate their children. In this way, the new meritocracy can perpetuate itself to a certain extent: an able child from a wealthy home can succeed far more rapidly than his poorer counterpart. Wealth is also used indiscriminately to further political ends. It would be almost impossible to become the leader of a democracy without massive financial backing. Money is as powerful a weapon as ever it was.

In societies wholly dedicated to the principle of social equality, privileged private education is forbidden. But even here people are rewarded according to their abilities. In fact, so great is the need for skilled workers that the least able may be neglected. Bright children are carefully and expensively trained to become future rulers. In the end, all political ideologies boil down to the same thing: class divisions persist whether you are ruled by a feudal king or an educated peasant.

The argument: key words

1. Nonsense about 'classless society', 'age of common man'.
2. Arguments: monarchy as system of government discredited; no political power.
3. Inherited wealth reduced by taxation; will disappear in time.
4. Some countries: the people rule; millenium, a reality.
5. These arguments are questionable.
6. Fallacies: all men are equal; society levelled out by equal educational opportunities.
7. (Can there ever be equal educational opportunities?)
8. Nature disregards the equality principle when dispensing brains, ability.
9. Rules of jungle: survival of fittest, might is right.
10. Education destroyed old class system, created new one; not aristocracy, but meritocracy.
11. Material rewards for genuine ability, skill, etc.
12. People use wealth to help their children: 'good start' – not considered wrong.
13. Private schools: in a democracy, free to choose.
14. Meritocracy self-perpetuating: ability plus wealth: more rapid success.
15. Wealth used for political ends; financial backing necessary for power.
16. Private education forbidden in some societies, but rewards still according to ability.
17. Great need for skilled workers, therefore least able neglected; bright children trained to rule.
18. Still class divisions whether under feudal king or educated peasant.

The counter-argument: key words

1. What is criterion of classless society? Freedom to compete for any position.
2. Impossible under old hereditary class system.
3. Quite possible today: a truly classless society.
4. External things (possessions, manner of dress, accent, behaviour, etc.) count for little.
5. Ability the important thing.
6. This hasn't created a new class: no rigid divisions in society.
7. Impossible for meritocracy to be self-perpetuating.
8. Social welfare systems widespread: east and west.
9. Social services available in many countries: health, education, pensions, etc.
10. Rights of individual safe-guarded: e.g. Ombudsman system in some countries.
11. Difficult for individual to become rich because of tax laws.
12. Surviving 'privileges' (monarchies, private schools, etc.) under constant attack.
13. Twentieth century *is* age of common man: his voice is the most powerful; Trade Unions, etc.
14. Highest ideals in our time: to further the *common* good, not the interest of a small class.

26 'No one wants to live to be a hundred'

It's only natural to look forward to something better. We do it all our lives. Things may never really improve, but at least we always hope they will. It is one of life's great ironies that the longer we live, the less there is to look forward to. Retirement may bring with it the fulfilment of a lifetime's dreams. At last there will be time to do all the things we never had time for. From then on, the dream fades. Unless circumstances are exceptional, the prospect of growing really old is horrifying. Who wants to live long enough to become a doddering wreck? Who wants to revert to that most dreaded of all human conditions, a second childhood?

Well, it seems that everybody wants to. The Biblical span of three score years and ten is simply not enough. Medical science is doing all it can to extend human life and is succeeding brilliantly. Living conditions are so much better, so many diseases can either be prevented or cured that life expectation has increased enormously. No one would deny that this is a good thing – provided one enjoys perfect health. But is it a good thing to extend human suffering, to prolong life, not in order to give joy and happiness, but to give pain and sorrow? Take an extreme example. Take the case of a man who is so senile he has lost all his faculties. He is in hospital in an unconscious state with little chance of coming round, but he is kept alive by artificial means for an indefinite period. Everyone, his friends, relatives and even the doctors agree that death will bring release. Indeed, the patient himself would agree – if he were in a position to give voice to his feelings. Yet everything is done to perpetuate what has become a meaningless existence.

The question of euthanasia raises serious moral issues, since it implies that active measures will be taken to terminate human life. And this is an exceedingly dangerous principle to allow. But might it not be possible to compromise? With regard to senility, it might be preferable to let nature take its course when death will relieve suffering. After all, this would be doing no more than was done in the past, before medical science made it possible to interfere with the course of nature.

There are people in Afghanistan and Russia who are reputed to live to a ripe old age. These exceptionally robust individuals are just getting into their stride at 70. Cases have been reported of men over 120 getting married and having children. Some of these people are said to be over 150 years old. Under such exceptional conditions, who wouldn't want to go on living forever? But in our societies, to be 70, usually means that you are old; to be 90, often means that you are decrepit. The instinct for self-preservation is the strongest we possess. We cling dearly to life while we have it and enjoy it. But there always comes a time when we'd be better off dead.

The argument: key words

1. We always look forward to something better.
2. One of life's ironies: the longer we live, the less to look forward to.
3. Retirement: fulfilment lifetime's ambitions.
4. From then on, dream fades; prospect growing old: horrifying.
5. Who wants to become doddering wreck? Revert to second childhood?

6. Everybody. Biblical span not enough.
7. Medical science, living conditions, etc., increased life expectation.
8. A good thing, provided we enjoy perfect health.
9. But is it a good thing to extend life to give pain, sorrow?
10. E.g. old man: lost all faculties; hospital, unconscious; kept alive artificial means; death: release; but meaningless existence prolonged.

11. Euthanasia: serious moral issues.
12. Deliberate termination life: a dangerous principle.
13. Compromise: let nature take its course; death relieve suffering.
14. As was done before medical progress.

15. Afghanistan, Russia: people reputed live very long time.
16. Robust at 70; marriage, children at 120; live to over 150.
17. Exceptional conditions: want to live forever.
18. But in our societies: 70: old; 90: decrepit.
19. Strong instinct self-preservation; but always time when we'd be better off dead.

The counter-argument: key words

1. As long as there's hope, possibility of life, man clings to it: natural tendency.
2. Care of the aged: the mark of a civilised society.
3. Many examples of success of modern medical science. E.g. Heart transplants; spare-parts surgery.
4. Why? People desperately want to go on living; most basic of human rights.

5. Even most infirm state is better than no life at all.
6. We haven't right to take decisions about others' lives.
7. Do we want others to take decisions about our lives?
8. The duty of science to prolong life: has always been so.
9. To do otherwise is first step to acceptance of euthanasia.
10. Allowing nature to take its course: a dangerous anti-life principle that can apply irrespectively to young and old.
11. E.g. would you let sick baby, young man, woman die because they are suffering?
12. Suffering is universal: can't have different rules for old and young.

13. People rarely think of death; take life for granted; *assume* they will live to 100.
14. They assume it because they want it.

27 'Capital punishment is the only way to deter criminals'

Perhaps all criminals should be required to carry cards which read: Fragile: Handle With Care. It will never do, these days, to go around referring to criminals as violent thugs. You must refer to them politely as 'social misfits'. The professional killer who wouldn't think twice about using his cosh or crowbar to batter some harmless old lady to death in order to rob her of her meagre life-savings must never be given a dose of his own medicine. He is in need of 'hospital treatment'. According to his misguided defenders, society is to blame. A wicked society breeds evil – or so the argument goes. When you listen to this kind of talk, it makes you wonder why we aren't all criminals. We have done away with the absurdly harsh laws of the nineteenth century and this is only right. But surely enough is enough. The most senseless piece of criminal legislation in Britain and a number of other countries has been the suspension of capital punishment.

The violent criminal has become a kind of hero-figure in our time. He is glorified on the screen; he is pursued by the press and paid vast sums of money for his 'memoirs'. Newspapers which specialise in crime-reporting enjoy enormous circulations and the publishers of trashy cops and robbers stories or 'murder mysteries' have never had it so good. When you read about the achievements of the great train robbers, it makes you wonder whether you are reading about some glorious resistance movement. The hardened criminal is cuddled and cosseted by the sociologists on the one hand and adored as a hero by the masses on the other. It's no wonder he is a privileged person who expects and receives VIP treatment wherever he goes.

Capital punishment used to be a major deterrent. It made the violent robber think twice before pulling the trigger. It gave the cold-blooded poisoner something to ponder about while he was shaking up or serving his arsenic cocktail. It prevented unarmed policemen from being mowed down while pursuing their duty by killers armed with automatic weapons. Above all, it protected the most vulnerable members of society, young children, from brutal sex-maniacs. It is horrifying to think that the criminal can literally get away with murder. We all know that 'life sentence' does not mean what it says. After ten years or so of 'good conduct', the most desperate villain is free to return to society where he will live very comfortably, thank you, on the proceeds of his crime, or he will go on committing offences until he is caught again. People are always willing to hold liberal views at the expense of others. It's always fashionable to pose as the defender of the under-dog, so long as you, personally, remain unaffected.

Did the defenders of crime, one wonders, in their desire for fair-play, consult the victims before they suspended capital punishment? Hardly. You see, they couldn't, because all the victims were dead.

The argument: key words

1. Criminals should carry cards: Fragile: Handle With Care.
2. We mustn't refer to them as thugs, but as social misfits.
3. Killer who murders old lady for savings needs 'hospital treatment'.
4. 'Society is to blame' argument – why aren't we all criminals?
5. We have done away with absurdly harsh laws: that's enough.
6. Suspension of capital punishment: senseless.
7. Violent criminal: a hero figure.
8. Glorified on screen and by press.
9. Great demand for crime stories.
10. Train robbers: a glorious resistance movement?
11. Cuddled by sociologists, adored by masses, the criminal is a privileged person.
12. He expects and receives VIP treatment.
13. Capital punishment was once a major deterrent: the robber, the poisoner.
14. It protected unarmed policemen, young children.
15. Now the criminal can get away with murder.
16. 'Life sentence': ten years 'good conduct' and then freedom to live on the proceeds of crime.
17. People hold liberal views at the expense of others.
18. Were victims consulted before suspension of capital punishment? No: they were dead.

The counter-argument: key words

1. We shouldn't be blinded by emotional arguments: glorification of criminal on screen, etc., irrelevant.
2. What are the facts? E.g. in Britain capital crime has *not* increased since suspension of capital punishment.
3. This has been proved many times in the past: relaxation of harsh laws has never led to increase in crime.
4. Therefore the 'deterrent' argument is absurd: capital punishment never protected anyone.
5. Those in favour of capital punishment are motivated only by desire for revenge and retaliation.
6. There has been a marked trend in society towards the humane treatment of less fortunate members.
7. E.g. compare the treatment of the insane in the past with today.
8. This same attitude characterises our approach to crime.
9. Hanging, electric chairs, garotting, etc., are barbaric practices, unworthy of human beings.
10. Suspension of capital punishment is enlightened and civilised.
11. Capital punishment creates, it does not solve problems.
12. Solution lies elsewhere: society *is* to blame.
13. Overcrowding, slums, poverty, broken homes: these are the factors that lead to crime.
14. Crime can only be drastically reduced by the elimination of social injustices – not by creating so-called 'deterrents' when the real problems remain unsolved.

28 'The space race is the world's biggest money waster'

Almost ever day we see something in the papers about the latest exciting developments in the space race. Photographs are regularly flashed to the earth from thousands and even millions of miles away. They are printed in our newspapers and shown on our television screens as a visible proof of man's newest achievements. The photographs neatly sum up the results of these massive efforts to 'conquer space' and at the same time they expose the absurdity of the undertaking. All we can see is an indistinguishable blob which is supposed to represent a planet seen from several thousand miles away. We are going to end up with a little moon-dust and a few stones which will be put behind glass in some museum. This is hardly value for money when you think that our own earth can provide countless sights which are infinitely more exciting and spectacular.

The space race is not simply the objective search for knowledge it is often made out to be. It is just an extension of the race for power on earth. Only the wealthiest nations can compete and they do so in the name of pure scientific research. But in reality, all they are interested in is power and prestige. They want to impress us, their spectators, with a magnificent show of strength. Man has played the power game ever since he appeared on earth. Now he is playing it as it has never been played before. The space race is just another aspect of the age-old argument that 'might is right'.

We are often told that technological know-how, acquired in attempting to get us into orbit, will be utilised to make life better on earth. But what has the space race done to relieve the suffering of the earth's starving millions? In what way has it raised the standard of living of any one of us? As far as the layman is concerned, the practical results of all this expenditure of money and effort are negligible. Thanks to space research, we can now see television pictures transmitted live half-way across the globe and the housewife can use non-stick frying-pans in the kitchen. The whole thing becomes utterly absurd when you think that no matter what problems man overcomes, it is unlikely that he will ever be able to travel even to the nearest star.

Poverty, hunger, disease and war are man's greatest enemies and the world would be an infinitely better place if the powerful nations devoted half as much money and effort to these problems as they do to the space race. For the first time in his history, man has the overwhelming technological resources to combat human suffering, yet he squanders them on meaningless pursuits.

If a man deprived himself and his family of food in order to buy and run a car, we would consider him mad. Individuals with limited budgets usually get their priorities right: they provide themselves with necessities before trying to obtain luxuries. Why can't great nations act in the same sensible way? Let us put our house in order first and let space look after itself.

The argument: key words

- 1 Space race achievements, always in news.
- 2 Photographs regularly in newspapers, on TV.
- 3 Visible proof of man's achievements.
- 4 Photographs sum up massive efforts to conquer space: absurd undertaking.
- 5 We see indistinguishable blob: a planet.
- 6 End up with moon-dust in museum; earth: more spectacular sights.

- 7 Space race: not objective search for knowledge but power race.
- 8 Wealthiest nations only: power and prestige.
- 9 Playing age-old power game as never before: 'might is right'.

- 10 We are told: technological know-how: improves life on earth.
- 11 Space race done nothing for starving millions.
- 12 Has not raised anyone's living standards.
- 13 Practical results negligible: TV, non-stick frying-pans.
- 14 Impossible ever to reach nearest star.

- 15 Greatest enemies: poverty, hunger, disease, war.
- 16 Money should be spent preventing these, not wasted on space race.

- 17 Individuals get their priorities right: e.g. car.
- 18 Necessities before luxuries.
- 19 Great nations: put our house in order first.

The counter-argument: key words

- 1 We cannot impose restrictions on man's desire for knowledge.
- 2 If we did: no progress.
- 3 E.g. progress in communications, travel, automation: all results of man's desire for knowledge.
- 4 Man ready technologically for space research, cannot do otherwise.

- 5 Man's intense curiosity: world fully explored; space is next logical step.
- 6 Even desire for prestige has its value: added incentive, greater efforts.
- 7 There are other ways of putting our house in order; no reason to give up space research.
- 8 Technology is already solving practical problems: e.g. protein obtained from oil and coal.

- 9 Space research fires imagination; very exciting achievements.
- 10 Satellites, Telstar, Moon, Venus, Mars.
- 11 Radio telescopes, satellite tracking, quasars.

- 12 There is no such thing as useless knowledge.
- 13 Increasing understanding of universe, earth, our origins.
- 14 Unforeseeable practical results.
- 15 Mass-emigration from overpopulated earth, a possibility?
- 16 Most exciting possibility of all: communication with other beings.

29 'Violence can do nothing to diminish race prejudice'

In some countries where racial prejudice is acute, violence has so come to be taken for granted as a means of solving differences, that it is not even questioned. There are countries where the white man imposes his rule by brute force; there are countries where the black man protests by setting fire to cities and by looting and pillaging. Important people on both sides, who would in other respects appear to be reasonable men, get up and calmly argue in favour of violence – as if it were a legitimate solution, like any other. What is really frightening, what really fills you with despair, is the realisation that when it comes to the crunch, we have made no actual progress at all. We may wear collars and ties instead of war-paint, but our instincts remain basically unchanged. The whole of the recorded history of the human race, that tedious documentation of violence, has taught us absolutely nothing. We have still not learnt that violence never solves a problem but makes it more acute. The sheer horror, the bloodshed, the suffering mean nothing. No solution ever comes to light the morning after when we dismally contemplate the smoking ruins and wonder what hit us.

The truly reasonable men who know where the solutions lie are finding it harder and harder to get a hearing. They are despised, mistrusted and even persecuted by their own kind because they advocate such apparently outrageous things as law enforcement. If half the energy that goes into violent acts were put to good use, if our efforts were directed at cleaning up the slums and ghettos, at improving living-standards and providing education and employment for all, we would have gone a long way to arriving at a solution. Our strength is sapped by having to mop up the mess that violence leaves in its wake. In a well-directed effort, it would not be impossible to fulfil the ideals of a stable social programme. The benefits that can be derived from constructive solutions are everywhere apparent in the world around us. Genuine and lasting solutions are always possible, providing we work within the framework of the law.

Before we can even begin to contemplate peaceful co-existence between the races, we must appreciate each other's problems. And to do this, we must learn about them: it is a simple exercise in communication, in exchanging information. 'Talk, talk, talk,' the advocates of violence say, 'all you ever do is talk, and we are none the wiser.' It's rather like the story of the famous barrister who painstakingly explained his case to the judge. After listening to a lengthy argument the judge complained that after all this talk, he was none the wiser. 'Possibly, my Lord,' the barrister replied, 'none the wiser, but surely far better informed.' Knowledge is the necessary prerequisite to wisdom: the knowledge that violence creates the evils it pretends to solve.

The argument: key words

1. In countries where racial prejudice is acute, violence is taken for granted.
2. E.g. white man rules by brute force; black man protests: fire and pillaging.
3. Important people on both sides see violence as a legitimate solution.
4. It's frightening to realise that man has made no progress: collars and ties instead of war-paint, but unchanged.
5. Recorded history has taught us nothing.
6. Violence only makes problem more acute: horror, bloodshed are not solutions.
7. Truly reasonable men don't get a hearing.
8. They advocate law enforcement and are mistrusted and persecuted.
9. Energy should be directed at clearing up slums, ghettos, improving living-standards, providing education, employment.
10. Strength sapped by violence.
11. Well-directed efforts: great benefits.
12. We must always work within the framework of the law.
13. First step: we must appreciate each other's problems.
14. An exercise in communication, exchanging information.
15. 'Talk, talk, talk, and we are none the wiser' – say advocates of violence.
16. Story of barrister and judge.
17. None the wiser. Possibly ... but far better informed.
18. Knowledge, the prerequisite of wisdom: the knowledge that violence creates the evils it pretends to solve.

The counter-argument: key words

1. What are the lessons about democracy which the black man has learnt from the white man? What has he learnt about liberty, equality and fraternity?
2. He has learnt that universal suffrage is a myth; that there are many forms of justice; that his presence devalues property.
3. Above all, he has learnt that the *status quo* is preserved by violence.
4. When dealing with each other, white men depend on force.
5. E.g. Peaceful co-existence between east and west is maintained by the constant threat of war.
6. Weakness on one side means domination by the other.
7. Weak opponents are repressed by force and kept in subjection by violence.
8. The black man has learned the rules of the game and applies them.
9. The Christian ideal of turning the other cheek is something the white man preaches but fails to practise.
10. The white man sets all the examples.
11. The *only* way to get a hearing is through violence.
12. Violence improves your status, encourages others to respect you as a force to be reckoned with.
13. Only then can the parties negotiate on equal terms.
14. Violence is a well-tried means of achieving peace and can succeed where other means are bound to fail.

30 'The most important of all human qualities is a sense of humour'

Biologically, there is only one quality which distinguishes us from animals: the ability to laugh. In a universe which appears to be utterly devoid of humour, we enjoy this supreme luxury. And it *is* a luxury, for unlike any other bodily process, laughter does not seem to serve a biologically useful purpose. In a divided world, laughter is a unifying force. Human beings oppose each other on a great many issues. Nations may disagree about systems of government and human relations may be plagued by ideological factions and political camps, but we all share the ability to laugh. And laughter, in turn, depends on that most complex and subtle of all human qualities: a sense of humour. Certain comic stereotypes have a universal appeal. This can best be seen from the world-wide popularity of Charlie Chaplin's early films. The little man at odds with society never fails to amuse no matter which country we come from. As that great commentator on human affairs, Dr Samuel Johnson, once remarked, 'Men have been wise in very different modes; but they have always laughed in the same way.'

A sense of humour may take various forms and laughter may be anything from a refined tinkle to an earthquaking roar, but the effect is always the same. Humour helps us to maintain a correct sense of values. It is the one quality which political fanatics appear to lack. If we can see the funny side, we never make the mistake of taking ourselves too seriously. We are always reminded that tragedy is not really far removed from comedy, so we never get a lop-sided view of things.

This is one of the chief functions of satire and irony. Human pain and suffering are so grim; we hover so often on the brink of war; political realities are usually enough to plunge us into total despair. In such circumstances, cartoons and satirical accounts of sombre political events redress the balance. They take the wind out of pompous and arrogant politicians who have lost their sense of proportion. They enable us to see that many of our most profound actions are merely comic or absurd. We laugh when a great satirist like Swift writes about war in *Gulliver's Travels*. The Lilliputians and their neighbours attack each other because they can't agree which end to break an egg. We laugh because we are meant to laugh; but we are meant to weep too. It is no wonder that in totalitarian regimes any satire against the Establishment is wholly banned. It is too powerful a weapon to be allowed to flourish.

The sense of humour must be singled out as man's most important quality because it is associated with laughter. And laughter, in turn, is associated with happiness. Courage, determination, initiative – these are qualities we share with other forms of life. But the sense of humour is uniquely human. If happiness is one of the great goals of life, then it is the sense of humour that provides the key.

The argument: key words

1. Biologically, ability to laugh distinguishes us from animals.
2. Universe devoid of humour; laughter a luxury; no biologically useful purpose.
3. Laughter: a unifying force.
4. Divided world; nations disagree; ideological factions; political camps; but everyone can laugh.
5. Laughter depends on sense of humour.
6. Certain comic stereotypes: universal appeal; e.g. Chaplin's films; little man versus society.
7. Dr Johnson: men wise, different modes; laughed same way.
8. Sense of humour and laughter: various forms: refined tinkle; earth-quaking roar.
9. Effect the same: maintaining sense of values.
10. Political fanatics lack humour.
11. Prevents us taking ourselves too seriously; reminds us: tragedy, comedy related.
12. Function of irony and satire.
13. Much grimness in world; cartoons, etc., redress balance.
14. Deflate arrogant politicians; show absurdity of actions.
15. E.g. Swift: *Gulliver's Travels*: Lilliputians: egg.
16. Satire banned in totalitarian regimes.
17. Sense of humour important; associated laughter, happiness.
18. Share some qualities with other forms life: e.g. courage, etc.
19. Sense of humour uniquely human.
20. Happiness: goal; sense of humour, key to happiness.

The counter-argument: key words

1. All human qualities are important.
2. It's absurd to stress one quality at the expense of others.
3. The ability to laugh is universal, but the sense of humour differs from country to country.
4. E.g. Cartoons, jokes of one nation not always funny to another.
5. Examples from humorous publications: *Punch, New Yorker, Krokodil,* etc.
6. Satire and irony can be harsh and cruel, not at all funny.
7. Humour emphasises less serious aspects of human life, therefore not so important.
8. Human achievements result from other qualities.
9. E.g. curiosity, ambition, imagination, intelligence, etc.
10. Humour does not solve any problems, merely blinds us to them.
11. Humour cannot alleviate suffering, etc.
12. Love, charity, compassion far more important.
13. Humour: not the key to happiness.
14. Happiness results from the combination of a great many qualities.

Forty additional topics

1. It is foolish to give money to beggars.
2. Duelling is a sensible way of settling an argument.
3. Men are worse gossips than women.
4. Women are only interested in getting married.
5. It is wrong to inherit money.
6. Relations are a nuisance.
7. Christmas should be abolished.
8. Animals should not be kept in captivity.
9. Parents should be sent to school.
10. The good old days were not good enough.
11. Learning to play a musical instrument is a waste of time.
12. Life begins at forty.
13. Crime pays very well.
14. Vegetarians have found the secret of good living.
15. Social change can best be achieved by revolution.
16. We wish the present government many happy returns.
17. It is right to meddle with Nature.
18. The churches and all they stand for are out of touch with modern life.
19. Too much knowledge is a dangerous thing.
20. Each country has the newspapers it deserves.
21. The United States of Europe is a fine ideal.
22. 'Manners maketh man.'
23. Men with moustaches have evil intentions.
24. The work done behind the scenes is what counts.
25. Hypocrisy is a virtue.
26. The Classics are boring.
27. The end of the world is at hand.
28. We have too much leisure.
29. We hope teaching-machines will replace teachers.
30. Maintaining an intelligence service is an old-fashioned idea.
31. Psychologists and psychiatrists are frauds.
32. The remaining monarchies should be allowed to die a natural death.
33. Civil servants should learn to be more civil.
34. The customer is always right.
35. School and university holidays are too long.
36. Exploring the past is a purposeless activity.
37. Saving money is painful and unnecessary.
38. Emigration will solve our problems.
39. It's not foolish to believe in ghosts.
40. We prefer brains to brawn.